The Castle Lectures in Ethics, Politics, and Economics

ROBERT B. PIPPIN

Hollywood Westerns and American Myth

The Importance of Howard Hawks and John Ford for Political Philosophy

Yale

UNIVERSITY

PRESS

NEW HAVEN AND LONDON

Published with assistance from the foundation established in memory of Calvin Chapin of the Class of 1788, Yale College.

Set in New Aster type by Westchester Book Co.
Printed in the United States of America.

Library of Congress Cataloging-in-Publication Data

Pippin, Robert B., 1948–
    Hollywood westerns and American myth : the importance of Howard Hawks and John Ford for political philosophy / Robert B. Pippin.
        p. cm. — (Castle lectures in ethics, politics, and economics)
    Includes bibliographical references and index.
    ISBN 978-0-300-14577-9 (cloth : alk. paper)
    1. Western films—History and criticism.   2. National characteristics, American, in motion pictures.   3. Politics in motion pictures.   4. Hawks, Howard, 1896–1977—Criticism and interpretation.   5. Ford, John, 1894–1973—Criticism and interpretation.   I. Title.

PN1995.9.W4P53 2010
791.43'6278—dc22   2009031174

A catalogue record for this book is available from the British Library.

This paper meets the requirements of ANSI/NISO Z39.48–1992 (Permanence of Paper).

10 9 8 7 6 5 4 3 2 1

THE CASTLE LECTURES

Parts of this book were given as the Castle Lectures in Yale's Program in Ethics, Politics, and Economics, delivered by Robert Pippin at Yale University in 2008.

The Castle Lectures were endowed by Mr. John K. Castle. They honor his ancestor the Reverend James Pierpont, one of Yale's original founders. Given by established public figures, Castle Lectures are intended to promote reflection on the moral foundations of society and government and to enhance understanding of ethical issues facing individuals in our complex modern society.

For Michael Fried and Jim Conant

CONTENTS

ACKNOWLEDGMENTS

I AM very grateful to Yale University, to the Program in Ethics, Politics, and Economics there, and to Seyla Benhabib for the invitation to give the Castle Lectures in 2008 (and for the program's willingness to permit me such an unusual approach to issues in political philosophy), and I am grateful for discussions about the topics with faculty and students at Yale. I have discussed the issues in the book with a number of individuals and audiences over the past year and a half and profited a great deal from these discussions at the Einstein Forum in Berlin, Catholic University, the University of Binghamton, Miami University of Ohio, the California College of the Arts, Indiana University, Georgetown University, the University of North Carolina, Sarah Lawrence College, and the Wissenschaftskolleg zu Berlin. I am especially grateful as well to Bob von Hallberg for encouraging me to give the series at Chicago (which I did in May 2008) and for supporting such a series, and to Greg Freeman and Jonny Thakkar for their help in the organization and publicity for those lectures. I am very much indebted to the long, spirited discussions with colleagues and students that followed each of the lectures.

All of the work on this book was made possible by the Andrew W. Mellon Foundation, and I am happy to have yet another occasion to thank the foundation for its extraordinary generosity and its Distinguished Achievement Award. I owe a great deal as well to a number of people with whom I have discussed the issues in this book, all of whom made important and useful suggestions. I am especially grateful to Brendan Boyle, David Bromwich, John Carroll, Jim Conant, Raine Daston, Bo Earle, Michael Fried, Paul Friedrich, Bob Gooding-Williams, Tom Gunning, Miriam Hansen, Mark Jenkins, Dan Morgan, Glenn Most, Richard Neer, Thomas Pavel, Gil Perez, Victor Perkins, C. D. C. Reeve, Susan Wolf, Candace Vogler, Bob von Hallberg, and George Wilson. The book is dedicated to two of these interlocutors, my friends Michael Fried and Jim Conant. I cannot possibly describe the degree of indebtedness I feel to both for many years of conversation about the issues treated here and about many other related ideas, except to say that I could not have possibly written this book without their help and friendship. I owe a special debt to my former colleague Mark Wilson, who some thirty years ago disabused me of my Europhile prejudices about "art" films and introduced me to the wonders and depths of classic Hollywood cinema.

1   INTRODUCTION

I

J OHN Ford's first great Western, his 1939 *Stagecoach*, has a
simple enough plot. A group of seven strangers has to crowd
into a stagecoach in the town of Tonto and, for seven different
reasons, journey across dangerous Indian territory to the town
of Lordsburg. We are not far into the narrative before the reasonably attentive viewer begins to notice several signs of a far
greater ambition than that of a standard adventure story. For
one thing, the characters seem deliberately representative, and
deliberately matched and contrasted in a way that goes beyond
the colorfully psychological. There is a haughty, respectable, but
pompous banker, Gatewood (who is also a thief), and there is
his opposite number, a shady, shoots-people-in-the-back gambler, Hatfield (a former southern "gentleman" who is traveling on
the stage solely to act as the southern gentlewoman's protector),

who turns out to be genuinely chivalrous and capable of sacrifice and nobility. There is a meek, gentle, and respectable whiskey salesman, the absolute bourgeois Peacock (who turns out to be made of much sterner stuff than we appreciate at first), and he is paired with his all-time best customer, a disgraced alcoholic physician, Doc Boone (who can summon back his skill and dedication when the situation calls for them). There is a prostitute, Dallas, who by conventional movie logic should be wise with a heart of gold but who, in a brilliant turn by Claire Trevor, is a nervous, edgy, somewhat whiny and bitter woman (who, of course, finally *does* have a heart of gold), paired and contrasted with a genteel pregnant southern woman, Lucy Mallory, who is at first contemptuous of her lower-class traveling companion but who comes to appreciate the worth and dignity of Trevor's character, and even to admire her. So we have avatars of bourgeois rectitude and their "anti-bourgeois" companions: a spirits peddler, a banker and a loyal wife, and a drunk, a gambler, and a prostitute, and many of them come to transcend and even invert their early (and perhaps our) class prejudices. In the middle of it all (literally, in the cramped stagecoach, and figuratively, as the story's pivotal character) is John Wayne's ambiguous character, the Ringo Kid, who joins the group en route, escaped from jail and on a mission of private revenge that the sheriff, traveling with them, has pledged to stop. (Ringo had been sent to jail as a sixteen-year-old, framed by the Plummer brothers, the murderers of his father and brother.) Ford introduces him to the narrative

1.1

with a spectacular shot, zooming up and close in, of Ringo waiting by the side of the road (fig. 1.1). This revenge issue in itself, as
in many Westerns, elevates the plot, marking out a theme of elemental importance. The difference between mere private revenge
and the justice demanded by law is at least as old as Aeschylus's
Oresteia, and the introduction of this ancient question gives us
another clue about the point and the ambiguous ending of the
film. (The sheriff, the representative of law, fails to stop the revenge killing; he hardly even makes a serious try, actually, and
even aids the extralegal attempt by Ringo.)

Once we realize how archetypal rather than merely individual are the treatment of character and the theme of justice,
it becomes clear that the journey itself is just as representative.
The film has thrown together people from very different back-
grounds and from very different social and economic classes.
Most of them either must get to Lordsburg or cannot return to

Tonto; they are driven inexorably forward with the same force
and power as the stagecoach itself, an image that Ford uses to
propel the film at a compelling, often thrilling pace.[1] And this
setup clearly poses a familiar question about the United States:
can such a collection of people, without much common tradition or history, without much of what had been seen as the social conditions of nationhood, become in some way or other a
unity capable of something greater than the sum of its parts?
This turns out to be a question not just about social cooperation but about a higher and more complicated unity—something
like a political unity. In the film, votes are taken about whether
to go on, and political metaphors are frequent. (Dallas asks Doc
if her expulsion is legitimate, consistent with natural right:
"Haven't I any right to live? What have I done?" The banker
pontificates about the state of politics. The question of whether
Ringo should leave his grievances to the law is present throughout the film.) We come to realize that Ford is asking whether a
group of this sort could ever be said to form a nation. He reminds us, by including a southern ex-officer and a woman of the
Old South, that America failed catastrophically to succeed at its
first try at nationhood, and that this failure has left a bitter legacy, affecting for the coach riders even the question of what the
"rebellion" should be called. But at the heart of Ford's question
are the problems of class and social hierarchy in such a nation,
and so, by contrast, the quintessentially American political ideal
of equality, the (potentially) binding force of such a norm.

1.2

We are shown that there are very wide open spaces in this setting and, so it would appear, room to avoid such questions, room for some psychological and social distance between such political citizens (fig. 1.2). (There is, that is, the grandeur and emptiness of Monument Valley, but also its hostility, the indifference of nature to the puny human attempts at civilized life.) But fate has crammed the travelers together in an absurdly small coach, suggesting that the illusion of escape to isolated independence is just that—an illusion. Their being packed into the coach makes visually clear their necessarily common fate (fig. 1.3). The narrative mostly concerns, within this enforced dependence, the dissolution and growing lack of credibility of class and even putative moral distinctions. We get a mythic representation of the American aspiration toward a form of politically meaningful equality, a belief or aspiration that forms the strongest political bond, such as it is, among Americans.

1.3

In a way, the film seems almost designed to address Tocqueville's famous ambivalence about American egalitarianism.
Although Tocqueville once noted a "manly" egalitarianism, of
which he approved (*everyone* aspiring to "greatness"), he was
deeply uneasy about what he took to be the American and more
material version. As far as he could see, such a passion was too
close to envy and resentment and would prove the great Achilles heel of the American experiment, inclining Americans to
restrictions on liberty when inequalities emerged. Here is his
claim.

> But the human heart also nourishes a debased taste for
> equality, which leads the weak to want to drag the strong
> down to their level and which induces men to prefer
> equality in servitude to inequality in freedom. It is not
> that peoples with a democratic social state naturally
> scorn freedom; on the contrary they have an instinctive
> taste for it. But freedom is not the chief and continual

object of their desires; it is equality for which they feel an eternal love; they rush on freedom with quick and sudden impulses, but if they miss their mark they resign themselves to their disappointment; but nothing will satisfy them without equality, and they would rather die than lose it.[2]

Ford's film is a compelling visual alternative, a picture of an aspiration to equality that Tocqueville did not seem to understand well—a claim to *moral* equality, the equal dignity and worth, the "inestimable" value of each individual as such, as Kant put it, following Rousseau. For all the inequalities in talent and accomplishment, no human life can be said to be worth more than any other, because no price or measure of value can be fixed on human worth. In the film, the collapse of the elaborately staged pretense to hierarchy and the realization of this form of equality occurs at a way station where the southern gentlewoman gives birth to her baby, and the common, shared human aspirations to peace, health, and domestic intimacy, and the common frailty and finitude of the human body, are experienced by almost everyone in the party. (There is of course controversy about this. Some see Dallas as accepting a subservient role, catering to the gentlewoman Lucy; she is redeemed only because she accepts a traditional woman/mother/class role.[3] But the baby unites *all* of them, reminding everyone of some dimension of commonality and some common aspiration for familial life and security. Rather than serving Lucy, Dallas actually "becomes" the mother, holding the baby far more often, and in

1.4

some sense she shames the others by challenging their assumptions about her "whorishess.")

The push in the group toward a more egalitarian form of mutual acknowledgment comes from Ringo's somewhat naïve but morally motivated insistence on drawing Dallas back into the society that has expelled her, and finally as well from the peddler Peacock, who asks for "a little Christian charity one for the other." The banker is a hopeless windbag throughout; the agents of this realization are the doctor and the prostitute, agents of the (equally frail) body, one might say (fig. 1.4). (This view differs from the Jeffersonian idealization of frontier or yeoman democracy as the condition most responsible for a more egalitarian, less Europeanized [that is, class-conscious] society. Indeed, it is *in* a frontier town, in the achieved civilization, Tonto, that the stark class divisions have so clearly reappeared.)[4]

The film shows this in a way that continues the archetypal, representative framework suggested by many of its elements, and I am interested in the following in the nature of that framework (in this case a representative tale of the insubstantiality and unreality of class hierarchies). Moreover, within the ambitious Westerns' sweeping, mythic explorations of the fate of politics in America there is often a reflective, distancing, uneasy "resolution that is not really a resolution." In *Stagecoach*, everything moves toward a revenge killing that we are led to hope will be final and transformative. The bad guys will have been eliminated, and a new start, with a civilized political order, is possible. But that new order is also figured in the Ringo Kid's love for Dallas. And in a somewhat bizarre twist he does not seem to realize, ever, despite her best efforts to drag him through the world she lives in, that she is a prostitute. (This, of course, is left ambiguous. A case could be made that he knows, perhaps that he always really knew. In any event, even his professed naïveté is unique among all the characters in the film.)[5] Ringo also shows that he never becomes a fully integrated and committed member of this group. During the final Apache raid on the stagecoach, he saves, at great risk to everyone else, three precious bullets for his private revenge quest, and he lies brazenly to the sheriff. The possibility of hope for a truly new beginning, a genuinely political order under these conditions, seems to depend on a level of naïveté that borders on the ludicrous. Moreover, the group cannot establish a new homeland in the United States; they must "escape" to Mexico. (It seems almost as if America needs its own America, its own New World, if it is to continue to be America—obviously a doomed hope.) And among the closing lines of the movie is: "There's two more *saved* from the blessings of civilization."[6]

Moreover, the most concrete expression of the possibility of a transcendence of class barriers is clearly supposed to be the acknowledgment by Lucy Mallory that Dallas is not only "as good as she is" but perhaps better, in a humanist, Christian sense. So when the coach arrives in Lordsburg we are in effect set up for that acknowledgment, but Lucy refrains from a public acknowledgment when surrounded by the gentlewomen of the town, and even when alone with Dallas she cannot fully express her gratitude. "If there is ever anything I can do . . ." And she stops, and lowers her eyes. Dallas, again taking the much higher ground, simply says, "I know," as if she means, "I know that you want to do something, say something, but this promise of a morally equal society is, we both know, a fantasy, and that I can never be anything but an ex-whore. At least in this country." We are shown the promise of a reconciliation and a new moral order, but then also shown their unreality.

Stagecoach is not an anomaly, either in the work created by Ford or in many similar, equally ambitious Westerns. I want to explore that ambition in what follows and to do so I need to introduce and explain the terms of relevance for this essay: the "political," the problem of political psychology, the problem of mythic narration, and the relevance of great Westerns to the distinctly American imaginary.

II

The question of what makes a human association or a particular sort of question political is worth several books on its own. Politics has at least something to do with ruling and with obedience, and that means the use of coercion and violence. So some think the issue is: What, if anything, distinguishes the organized use of violence and coercion by one group of people against another from the exercise of power in everyone's name? Can someone really act as a "representative" in this way, and so not as an individual or group member? And of course there are also some very influential modern thinkers who claim that politics and political power are nothing but names for the mere pretense that such coercion is anything other than a strategy by a group or a class or a type to gain advantage over others. Marx famously claimed something like this; so, it appears, did Nietzsche.[7] For them there is no such thing as politics. Others think that while there *used* to be politics, there is not anymore. For them politics has come to mean the administrative, bureaucratic, and technological administration of the economic life of civil society, and not at all a deliberation in common about the common good, and so politics in this modern sense does not designate anything distinctive, as it used to. Hannah Arendt seems to believe something like this.[8]

The question is whether there is—especially in modern America—a unique sort of social bond that links individuals, often strangers, in a distinctive ethical relationship and distinctive sort of enterprise—citizenship. The question is the one raised by Rousseau's famous statement in 1750 in the *First Discourse:* "We have physicists, geometers, chemists, astronomers, poets, musicians, painters . . . we no longer have citizens."[9]

A traditional philosophical approach to this question would have it that this question is the same as: Are there good reasons for individuals to form such a distinctive social relation, to obligate themselves to sustain it? In much contemporary political philosophy this has meant that the basic question of politics has pretty much become the question of legitimacy, essentially the legitimacy of the state's claim to a monopoly on the use of legitimate coercive force. This is certainly an important issue, but it also represents quite a narrowing of focus when compared with the range of issues addressed by Plato or Machiavelli, or Hobbes or Rousseau or Hegel. In all these cases it is simply assumed that in order to answer the question about the best organization of ruling and ruled, about how we might best live in common, we must address the question of the human soul. This includes the question of what sort of soul is best suited for what sort of regime, and what sort of soul is likely to be produced by what sort of regime, as well as some position on the basic dynamics of the human soul, especially with regard to voluntary submission to some authority.

This claim about the relevance of political psychology to political philosophy assumes that there is something amiss in addressing the political question as if human beings were exclusively rational calculators or creatures of pure practical reason. We know, that is, that we are motivated in our political lives by quite a complex psychology, and we would not be doing justice to the questions of politics if we were to neglect the core political passions. These are usually identified as, among others, love, especially love of one's own, fear (fear of violent death, of suffering and insecurity), desire for ease and luxury and pleasure, and a powerful passion (perhaps the most problematic political passion) called by many names: *thymos, amour-propre*, vanity, self-love, the desire for recognition, the need to secure one's status with others and even to elevate one's status above and even at the expense of others. (As we shall see, this last proves the most difficult for commercial republics to contain or sublimate or suppress.) All the great political philosophers were concerned with how to understand the role of such passions in the practices of ruling and obeying. Some of these themes and a treatment of such themes are important in all three of the films I discuss here. In *Red River* the questions concern the charismatic nature of authority, the psychological glue in various sorts of social bonds, and the psychic costs of the unique forms of social cooperation and sacrifice demanded by modern societies. In *The Man Who Shot Liberty Valance* the psychological dimensions of American modernization are raised again, this time about the roles of imagination and fantasy in the possibility of political life and in the tensions between private and social passions. And in *The Searchers* some of the darkest aspects of the feelings of kinship, hatred, revenge, and self-deceit let loose by conflict and war are given a treatment with few equals in American literature.

Such reflections on political actuality are not irrelevant to political philosophy, and to the question of living well in common. That is, it need not always be the case that the lack of fit between a proposed ideal or rational structure and a dissatisfying experience of such demands in a life is a result of irrationality or evil. Things come to matter to people in all sorts of ways, and while it might not be rational, say, to love one person or group more than others and to act on that basis, such a differentiation need not at all be a flaw or failure, or just evidence that a scheme is impractical, that it might not work. Rather, it might be evidence that such a scheme is not desirable. A rational scheme is one thing; what it comes to mean in the actual lives of mortal, psychologically complex persons in some community at some time is another thing.[10]

The point is put well by the most prominent political philosopher of our time, John Rawls, often, despite the neglected third part of *A Theory of Justice,* classified as a political rationalist. "Conceptions of justice must be *justified* by the conditions of our life *as we know it* or not at all."[11] As we shall see, this formulation—the "conditions of *our* life as we *know* it"— introduces the deeper issue. What counts as "knowing" such conditions? How do we obtain such knowledge of "our" human condition relevant to politics?

With this in mind, let me just state the five main points that I would like to defend in this book. (i) Political psychology is essential to any worthwhile political philosophy. (ii) The sort of political psychology necessary cannot be properly understood as an empirical social science. (iii) It must reflect an understanding of the experiential or first-personal dimension of political experience, and that means it must involve a complex, historically inflected interpretive task. We need to know what matters to people at a place and time, why it matters, what matters more than other things (more than anything in some contexts), what they are willing to sacrifice for, what provokes intense anger, and so forth. And we will not learn this by relying on what as a matter of historical fact they say or said, nor by arbitrarily imputing to them one supreme motivation—the rational satisfaction of their preferences. (iv) Novels and films and other artworks are essential, not incidental or merely illustrative, elements of such a task. (v) Most controversially of all, such interpretive work, in raising the question of the political actuality within which political philosophy would have a point, is itself philosophical work, not illustrative or merely preliminary. Let me start by saying a little about the third and fourth points.

III

To be able to say anything of any generality about political passions, we also have to concede that they cannot be viewed as standard objects of study, accessible to a third-person or observational standpoint like many other objects. We can see what we take to be manifestations of indignation, anger, vanity, jealousy, and greed, but that is already an interpretive rather than observational claim, and we cannot actually ever see such passions. Our access to them is largely first-personal; we imagine what it is like to be such a subject at such a time in such a situation, and we add to such an imagined experience the more we know about the person's background—what else he does in other situations and, especially, with the appropriate caution, what he says.[12] Moreover, at the first-order level of political life, for actual participants decisions are made, commitments affirmed, sacrifices made, and the like, all in a way that would appear to be much more decisively oriented from and grounded in one's experiences, sometimes crisis experiences of fear, humiliation, resentment, pride, and so forth. So it would seem reasonable to try to get such experiences and their connection to political life in view, to try to interpret and understand them; at least as reasonable as wondering whether an argument can be found to justify some claim to the legitimate use of power.

Given this situation, I propose that we not limit ourselves to the situations and experiences imagined by a few philosophers, or to the historical examples many of them use, but rather expand our range of data to include, as relevant to (perhaps indispensable to) political reflection, aesthetic works of considerable complexity and ambiguity—works such as Shakespeare's history plays, novels by Tolstoy or Dickens or Coetzee, plays by Ibsen or Arthur Miller, and films. I shall assume that many twentieth-century films are the equal in aesthetic quality of any of these works in their ability to represent the fundamental problems of the human condition, especially our political condition and its psychological dimensions. If someone does not believe that, say, Renoir's *Grand Illusion*, Kurosawa's *Seven Samurai*, Kubrick's *Paths of Glory*, Welles's *Citizen Kane* or *The Magnificent Ambersons*, and many others belong on the list of these objects, then my argument here will seem supremely improbable, and I am afraid I will not be able to say much convincing about that issue in general. However, I will discuss three specific films and make the case for their relevance that way. For the films I want to consider are commercial Hollywood products, made by studios out to turn a profit and so aimed at mass audiences.[13]

IV

It is generally agreed that while over seven thousand Westerns have been made since the first Western, the silent *The Great Train Robbery* of 1903, it was not until the publication of two seminal articles in the fifties by André Bazin and Robert Warshow that the genre began to be taken seriously.[14] Indeed, Bazin argued that the "secret" of the extraordinary persistence of the Western must be due to the fact that the Western embodies the "essence of cinema," and he suggested that that essence was its incorporation of myth and mythic consciousness of the world. He appeared to mean by this that Westerns tended to treat characters as types and that the narrative revolved around a small number of essential plots offering various perspectives on fundamental issues faced by any society, especially the problem of law and political authority.[15] Bazin expressed great contempt for critics who thought that Western plots were "simple," and he insisted that the right way to understand such simplicity was by reference to the "ethics" of epic and tragic literature; he called the great French playwright Corneille to mind as a worthy forerunner. The Western, he said, turned the Civil War into our Trojan War, and "the migration West is our Odyssey." (One could go even further, paraphrasing a German commentator: the Greeks had their *Iliad;* the Jews the Hebrew Bible; the Romans the *Aenead;* the Germans the *Nibelungenlied;* the Scandinavians their *Sagas;* the Spanish the *Cid;* the British the Arthurian legends. The Americans have John Ford.)[16]

Mythic accounts are about events in the remote past of decisive significance for the present (often about foundings), and they assume that the course of these events is the result of actions undertaken by heroes of superhuman abilities. The tone is one of elevated seriousness, so the form of such mythic storytelling is usually epic.[17] This elevation of Westerns (or the handful of great ones among that seven thousand) into epic literature with mythical heroes and events was not of course universally accepted. The idea of a "bourgeois epic," or the idea that commercial republics could have an epic dimension, can seem faintly comic, and I will return to this issue frequently. Some commentators saw many Westerns of the 1950s as mostly about cold war politics, or argued that their appeal could be explained by reference to the fantasies of white working-class male adolescents, or insisted on their essentially deformed, masculine, patriarchal (and so hardly universal) perspective, or claimed that no progress would be made until we included the Western within a general theory of cinematic pleasure, usually a psychoanalytic theory.[18] But when this mythic notion was combined, as it frequently was, with Frederick Jackson Turner's famous frontier hypothesis in his influential essay "The Significance of the Frontier in American History" (that many aspects of something like

an American national character could be understood by reference to the experience of the frontier and the expansion West,
the long struggle, so vivid in our national memory, of "a place
where advancing civilization met declining savagery"[19]), such an
interpretive frame became an even more powerful one.[20]

I shall adopt a version of it here in the pursuit of this theme
of political psychology. For many great Westerns are indeed
about the founding of modern bourgeois, law-abiding, property-
owning, market-economy, technologically advanced societies in
transition—in situations of, mostly, lawlessness (or corrupt and
ineffective law) that border on classic "state of nature" theories.
The question often raised is that of how legal order (of a particular form, the form of liberal democratic capitalism) is possible,
under what conditions it can be formed and command allegiance, how the bourgeois virtues, especially the domestic virtues, *can be said to get a psychological grip in an environment
where the heroic and martial virtues are so important.* To say that,
however relevant to history, the narrative form is not historical
or realistic, but mythic, will be understood to mean seeing such
films as attempts to capture *the* fundamental problem in a
founding, the institution of law, or in some other way to capture
the core drama in a particular form of political life. With the
stakes raised so high, this also means that the heroes of such
dramas are indeed often super-heroic, near divinities. One man
can out-duel five others in a shoot-out (if you recall the "Achilles
and Patroclus" ending of *Unforgiven* or the final gunfight in

Stagecoach); a hero can be accurate with a pistol at two hundred yards, and so forth, just as Odysseus can slay all the suitors and Achilles can terrify an entire army with one war cry.[21] Accordingly, the acting styles and visual sweep are, in their grandiosity and ambition, much closer to opera than to filmed domestic dramas. (Not for nothing are they derisively known as "horse operas.")

It is also true of course that while these events are foundings they are also the results of imperialist colonization or even wars of extermination. Thus the way these societies remember or mythologize their foundings, and their attempts to do this consistent with their own pacific, Christian, and egalitarian self-image, will make for a serious and complicated problem.

Finally, the Westerns I am interested in are not purely or solely universalistic myths.[22] It is true that the narratives are not merely anecdotal; the films aspire to a form of universality—not the universality of scientific law or generalization but a universality consistent with the ineliminability of the first-person perspective, the universality of a common experience of a basic human problem, the political problem. They aspire to *mythic universality*. Although they retain a mythic form of narration they are also very much about America and the self-understanding of rapid American modernization in the West in the nineteenth century. Many classic plots involve the coming of sheepherders and farmers and railroads to what had been open range, and so the establishment of fences and the laying of track can provoke a great crisis. Others involve the attempt by a hero from the basically pre-modern, quasi-feudal world—an ex-gunfighter—to find a place in the new bourgeois, domestic world. He is in effect a figure (usually tragic) for the whole transition and modernity issue itself. (This is what obviously appealed to and inspired Kurosawa, who treated the samurai as the same kind of transitional figure at the end of the feudal period, with the same pathos and tragedy.) Presented mythically, the problem is the transition from the feudal patriarchal authority that arose in the pre-legal situation of the frontier to a more fraternal, modern form; and the films are about the psychic costs of such a transition. The arrival of the railroad, mining industries, the telegraph, the new role of banking, and so forth are often quite prominent. And of course there is concern, above all, with the rule of law over vigilante and strongman rule, and the question of how much of a difference this really is. (As Gilberto Perez puts it, "The reason the Western has the classic showdown between hero and villain take place on the main street of town is that the matter at stake is not a merely personal but a public, a social matter.")[23] In fact most great Westerns are in one way or another not about the opening and exploration of the frontier but about the so-called "end of the frontier," and that means in effect the end of the New Beginning that America had promised itself. America in the period covered by most Westerns, 1865 or so to 1890, is ceasing to be a land of promise and becoming a historical actuality like any European country, no longer a great, vast potentiality.[24]

America's geography made it possible for Americans to keep reenacting the core element of the American myth—a new beginning. The West became for Americans what America had been for Europeans, a fresh start and freedom from the decadence of old Europe, or of the "Europeanized," weak, clueless Easterners of many Westerns.[25] In the beginning of *Stagecoach*, in the town of Tonto, the prostitute and the alcoholic doctor are being evicted by the morally self-righteous (a group of ladies called the Law and Order League which seems designed to represent Tocqueville's "tyranny of the majority"), but at least the two of them have somewhere to go. It is somewhere wilder and more dangerous, but it is still a field of possibility. When Doc Boone explains to Dallas that the ladies are "scouring out the dregs of the town," he suggests in a way quite distinctly American: "Come, be a proud, glorified dreg like me."[26] (Hegel even thought that this geography allowed Americans a unique solution to modern social tensions—an ever-expanding colonization westward.[27] All of this had to come to an end at some point. There's only so much land.)

The Civil War also gets a mention in many Westerns, reminding us that this was the end of the plantation agrarian system that had defined so much of the American economy for so long, and that this war produced the bitter, violent, wandering southerners so much a staple of Western characters. The war theme also reminds us that with the failure, in effect, of our first attempt to form and sustain a new type of national unity we needed to hope for a national reconciliation—a "problem" of human spirit, not simply a problem of practical reason. We receive in many Westerns not just a mythic account of the founding of legal, civil society, with an American inflection, but the expression of a great anxiety about what this particular founded society will be like, whether it can hold together, whether it can really leave behind what it was. By this I mean leaving behind the mythic and largely feudal notion of nearly complete self-sufficiency and self-reliance, an honor code, the unavoidability of violence in establishing and maintaining proper status and order, a largely male and isolated world. Hence that familiar theme of ex-gunfighters trying to "go straight," to become bourgeois citizens, or the near-comic obsolescence of the gunfighter code in modern societies, as in Peckinpah's classics, *The Wild Bunch* or *Ride the High Country*. This issue returns us to the problem mentioned above. If we treat Westerns as a reflection on the possibility of modern, bourgeois domestic societies to sustain themselves, command allegiance and sacrifice, defend themselves from enemies, inspire admiration and loyalty (that is, to command and form the politically relevant passions in some successful way, to shape the "characters" distinctly needed for this form of life), then one surprising aspect of many Westerns (often criticized in the 1960s for their supposed chauvinism, patriarchy, celebration of violence, and so forth) is a profound *doubt* about the ability of modern societies (supposedly committed to peace and law) to do just that.[28] (Put another way, if we believe writers like Albert

Hirschman and many others, the central task in the founding of a modern political order was to find a way to denigrate, contain, and deemphasize the chief pre-modern mark of distinction, *glory*, with all the militaristic and violent and dangerous dimensions of that task, in favor of a more scientific view of the primacy of the fear of death and the desire for peace.)[29] The first two films under discussion, *Red River* and *The Man Who Shot Liberty Valance*, involve a multilayered reflection on what it would mean to submerge the drive to distinction, honor, glory, and aristocratic independence to the demands of security, cooperation, and peace. As we shall see, the record of such an embourgeoisement is an incomplete and vexed one in the American experience, as the bourgeois virtues also seem to involve such a commitment to security, life, and peace that hypocrisy, self-deceit, and a prosaic form of life perhaps incapable of sustaining the required deep allegiance seem an inevitable consequence.

2 *RED RIVER* AND THE RIGHT TO RULE

I

*R*ED *River* (Howard Hawks, 1948) has some tenuous connections with actual events—the founding of the vast King ranch in Texas and the creation of the Chisolm Trail. The film tells the story of how Tom Dunson (John Wayne), together with a long-time friend, a sort of comic, Sancho Panza character, Nadine Groot (Walter Brennan), and a foundling child, Matt Garth (Montgomery Clift, playing the foundling role that is an old mythic theme),[1] whom they took in after an Indian attack killed his parents, founded an immense cattle ranch in southwest Texas, near the Red River. Fourteen years later the collapse of the beef market in the South after the Civil War threatens to bankrupt the ranch. They have nine thousand cattle to sell but no market. So Tom and his crew, which now includes the adult Matt back from fighting in the war, prepare an extremely risky venture, a cattle drive all the way north to Missouri. We learn that others have tried this drive and all have failed, the victims of murderous bandits, Indian attacks, and the scale of the enterprise itself. (It is about a thousand miles and they can cover about ten miles a day, so their journey will be over three months long.) In the course of this drive Tom becomes more and more worried about their success and this leads him to become increasingly tyrannical and monomaniacal. (His character reminds one of a character in an equally epic account of an American founding, also with biblical undertones, Faulkner's Sutpen in *Absalom, Absalom!* who himself calls to mind what is in many ways the archetypal American "hero," and who clearly serves as a figure not only for Dunson but even more for Ethan in *The Searchers* and Ahab in Melville's *Moby-Dick*.) Eventually he seems close to madness, and when he wants to execute two "deserters" who have been hunted down and brought back, Matt rebels, mutinies, takes over the herd, and banishes Dunson, who swears revenge. The men back Matt, who decides to trust reports that have been filtering in that there is now a train link in Abilene, Kansas. They gamble that this is true and head there.[2] The reports turn out to be correct, and the cattle are sold at a great profit. But Tom *does* return, with a band of henchmen, and in one of the greatest Western scenes he stalks grimly through a cattle herd toward Matt to kill him. Matt refuses to draw his gun and they begin a fistfight.

We are led to expect that this will be a fight to the death because the epic framework invoked calls to mind so many such archetypal scenes in which the deposed father must die to make way for the son and the new order. Often he dies wiser, understanding how his old ways have led him to such a point, and at peace with the new age and the fact that he has no place in it.

But Tom does not die. A woman with whom Matt has fallen in love on the trail (in a very hastily arranged and somewhat clumsy plot development), Tess (Joanne Dru), arms herself and stops the fight, proclaiming in some anger that it has really been all a show, that anyone can see that they love each other, and she stalks off. There is a kind of jokey, heavily criticized fraternal scene between the men, and the film ends.

Although the framework of the film suggests an epic narration, this is a bit complicated. It is indeed a movie about a founding and a traditional founder-hero, and it deals with a common Western theme, the "coming of civilization." Therefore it raises both the transition issue and the problem of the persistent need for the violent suppression of disorder (eventually, in many movies, creating Plato's "who will guard the guardians?" problem).[3] And the title itself, suggestive of the Red Sea and Moses leading the Israelites out of Egypt, brings to mind a biblical epic. But the complications begin here.

There *is* something directly and symbolically epic about the cattle drive, fully visible in a fine scene when they recross the Red River, whose original crossing marked the beginning of the enterprise. It *is* an epically vast undertaking. There *is* something symbolically powerful in the attempt by mere mortals to "herd" and harness these potentially destructive, elemental natural forces, to bend nature to human will and found a civilized order. (The cattle stampede scene makes this point in grand style, and the cattle, with their swarming, massive, anonymous power, can suggest the forces of history itself.)[4] But this view of epic ambition and this sense of the grandeur of it all is the perspective eagerly accepted and promoted by Tom Dunson; it is *his* epic-heroic view of himself, and those who share that point of view (all Texans, then and now, no doubt). We shouldn't lose track of the fact that this effort is all about getting some cattle to market in order to preserve a commercial enterprise; it has nothing "Mosaic" to do with liberating an enslaved people.[5] However, it is not as if the epic and mythic dimensions of the enterprise are simply ironized—that would be going too far. But Howard Hawks, the director, and Borden Chase, the screenwriter, do not simply adopt or unqualifiedly encourage us to adopt Tom's view (or the "Texan" view or the "conventional" view). This unsettledness is one of the most interesting things about the film (and, as we shall see, about many Westerns).[6]

II

Consider three aspects of the way in which we are introduced to Tom's "quest." The uncertainty or unsettledness about perspective or point of view is immediately and strikingly apparent.

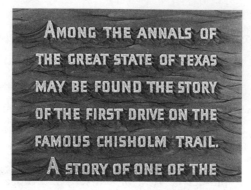

2.1

In the year 1851, Thomas Dunson accompanied by a friend, Nadine Groot, left St. Louis and joined a wagon train headed for California. Three weeks on the trail found them near the northern border of Texas. The land to the south looked good to

2.2

Note that there is both a written "movie version" of the introduction and scene-setting of the film and then an odd shift to another perspective, as if a different one, a book called *Tales of Early Texas* (figs. 2.1 and 2.2). The book is not even a published account, but handwritten, like a personal diary, adding to the idea of a subjective and limited point of view.

The more official-looking movie version does not purport simply to tell us what happened. We read that "*In the annals* of the great state of Texas may be found the story of the first drive on the famous Chisolm trail . . ." and not "Here is the story of the first drive . . .") As the book itself (perhaps the "annals" mentioned) opens, we in effect begin the story again, and then, adding to the complexity, the camera begins to pan in for a close-up then oddly *keeps* moving forward, too close here and elsewhere, whenever the intertitles appear, for the proper reading perspective. And the bottom left third or so is covered in shadow. Whenever this reminder that we are following a certain narrative, not seeing a dramatization of the facts, occurs, there are always such words outside the frame of the film, impossible to read properly because the camera is too close. There are fourteen such intertitle episodes.

Then the great opening scene: an epic vastness with a wagon train coming straight at us, and then an action that will define the core issue raised in the film. A wagon dramatically pulls out of line, Tom's (John Wayne's) wagon (fig. 2.3). We begin, in other words, with a mutiny or rebellion of sorts, a picture of individualist self-assertion, and the question is raised: When is such an act of mutiny or self-assertiveness justified?

That is, in effect, the first issue raised. In the first dialogue of the film, the confrontation between Tom and the wagon train leader, we are thrown into a complicated political issue that will return as the core of the drama itself, and it clearly

2.3

foreshadows the Civil War to come. Dunson announces that he is leaving the train before they reach their goal, and the question that is posed is a complicated one: Just what had Tom Dunson "consented" to do by joining the train in St. Louis and staying with it this far? People traveled in wagon trains because traveling alone was terribly more dangerous, and although, as Dunson says in a Philadelphia lawyerly way, he "did not sign anything," he enjoyed the extra security of the train for a long time, and it is quite clear he never mentioned to anyone: "As soon as I see some land I like, I'm going to stop." The leader is stunned by Tom's decision. He joined in St. Louis and they are now in northern Texas. That was a vast distance in those days, months of traveling, long enough for him and a woman we will see shortly, Fen (Coleen Gray), to fall in love and, as they used to say, to become bespoken. It is not at all unreasonable for this community, and Fen, to think of Dunson, having enjoyed their mutual protection for weeks upon weeks, as deserting them in their hour of need. (We will soon learn that it is indeed their direst hour; an Indian attack is imminent.) So Dunson's original founding act is shrouded in a moral ambiguity that is relevant to any political association that thinks of itself as founded on consent. It also provides a good deal of irony when, on the cattle drive, Dunson is given to speechifying about how he "hates quitters, especially when they are not good enough to finish what they start."

And then there is the strange issue of the "sexlessness" of the whole thing, the supposed impossibility of women in this new world. In a strange conversation with Fen, Dunson denies her permission to come along (thus unknowingly condemning her to death), and she pleads her case in a way that is unusually frank for 1948. She says, "I'm strong; I can stand anything you can." And when Tom insists that it will be "too much for a woman," she makes her strongest argument: "Put your arms around me, Tom. Hold me; feel me in your arms. Do I feel weak, Tom? I don't, do I? You'll need me; you'll need what a woman can give you to do what you have to do. Oh, listen to me, Tom . . . The sun only shines half the time, Tom; the other half is night" (fig. 2.4). It might seem that we have here a classic case of the "masculinist" perspective that Westerns have been criticized for, and there is something to that. That is, Dunson has epic ambitions, and we see acted out in front of us the fact that what we might consider the strongest private bond in the human world,

2.4

eros, here romantic love, is not powerful enough to qualify or compromise such ambition. But it becomes pretty clear pretty quickly that Tom was wrong in not taking Fen with him, both in a private and a politically symbolic sense. Groot tells him so rather bluntly when they learn of the attack and massacre, and that view seems to be the movie's perspective, too. As we shall see in other contexts, the issue being joined here is not sexual politics but the politics of founding and the idea of a self-generated (and so entitled) mini-empire, as if beholden to no one; autochthonous. Any such beholding is assumed to qualify the title to rule. And we shall see in many ways that *that* is wrong, too. We are clearly supposed to keep her words in mind. "Just once in your life, *change your mind*," she urges. This is something that Dunson, catastrophically, cannot do on the trail.

So several aspects of the story have been introduced: the perspective of the narration is not necessarily the "film's," as if an omniscient narrator's; we are, it is suggested, in some way "too close" to the narration, too invested, perhaps as Americans, in this heroic-epic version, to see it clearly; Dunson's own mutiny is not ethically unproblematic (perhaps no founding is);[7] and his vision of what he is to do—to generate his empire artificially, let us say, without women—and so his abandonment of the wagon train and Fen, seem extreme, off track.

This sexuality and artificiality or unnaturalness theme is continued, too. When Tom's party comes upon the young survivor, Matt, after the massacre and after their own fight with the Indians (during which the river is actually stained red with the blood of Native Americans), we discover that Tom has only one bull left, and no cow. Matt, whom they find wandering alone, has a cow, or he does duty in some way for the "female" side, and that suggests another complication in the relationship between Matt and Tom.[8] It is a theme that will recur: an important issue later on the drive is whether Matt is too soft or even too feminine to rule men and lead the drive. And again this is a perspective that the viewer should not assume is simply the film's. This point of view and the assumptions about Matt (and, given Tess's role at the end, about women) also turn out to be "wrong." It would be an independent theme to pursue here, but this generation image does seem to be connected to the psychological distortion in Tom's view of what he is doing—the fantasy of complete independence and almost autochthony, self-generation, of being beholden to no one—that leads him to this project in the first place and almost destroys it. (One might yet again call it a deeply American fantasy, connected with the "new beginning" and exceptionalism fantasy.) *Something* is off-key throughout the film in Tom's view of dependence and mutuality. The snake bracelet that was his mother's and that he gives to Fen and then to Matt, and which ends up on Tess's wrist at the end, often functions more like the brand he seems to want to put on everything. Put another way, Matt is only Dunson's adopted son, not his generated or natural son, just as America is an artificial, invented country willed into existence rather than "grown naturally" over several centuries. (Or *all* Americans are like adopted children, not organically produced by a "natural" country or nation state, a "motherland.")[9]

III

We are shown what are in effect two isolated instances of Tom's "founding acts," clearly meant to do duty for the whole issue. The first is the crossing of the Red River and the fight with the attacking Indians that ensues. Right by first possession is apparently supposed to yield to right by conquest, in the implied argument of the film, because the land is and has been multiply claimed. Second, Tom must also fight off neighboring Mexican claimants to the land who show up soon after he arrives. Two representatives of one Don Diego (who is "at home, six hundred

2.5

kilometers south") appear and politely but firmly tell Tom and his group that they are trespassing and must leave. This introduces another quasi-Lockean argument: "That's too much land for one man. Why, it ain't decent," says Groot, as if there is some natural justice determined by the amount of land one can productively make use of. We get back to the basic issues when Tom asks how Don Diego got the land. When told he was granted it by the king of Spain, Tom counters that this just means "he took it from whoever was here before," meaning Native Americans. We are clearly supposed to infer that it was always so, that some Indian tribe no doubt took it from whatever tribe was there before. The argument at this point runs out; Tom shoots one of the two envoys in a quick-draw duel (fig. 2.5).

Much later we learn that this was not the end of the story, and that many such fights have ensued in the fourteen years between this event and the start of the drive. We are shown seven graves in testimony to Tom's victory. This does not add up to a convincing argument for such colonial conquest, but our reactions are at least muted a bit, given that Tom took the land from an imperial power (and a European one, Europe and the East being familiar foils to the "new" Western way of life) and by the suggestion that since there has been nothing here but a succession of such violent conquests and defeats, there is nothing especially problematic in this one.

After all this private empire building, Tom ends up with nine thousand head of cattle and no market in the defeated South. The new problem is much more an economic one, and that has been caused by a political crisis. It is still the West, however, so the solution will require courage, hardiness, tenacity, and strength of will for the long drive, along with some understanding of the new situation and some way of managing it. (Groot tells Matt that Tom learned something new during the war, that a ranch "ain't only beef; it's money. He didn't know about money, Matt. He never had none." Matt's response is interesting. He says, "You mean he just doesn't know who to fight.") The political dimension reappears in the second invocation of contract and what contract means, an issue of great relevance to the civil war that ruined the beef market. The night before the big drive Tom lays out for the men how terribly risky the venture will be (no one has yet succeeded) and releases anyone who does not

2.6

want to take the chance, promising them no disgrace and all jobs when they return. A few family men leave. (Miraculously, on the drive itself they do not encounter any border bandits or Indians.) Tom insists on what he clearly wants to be a strict and sacred contract, something that will play a large role in the later mutiny (and in the issue of whether the bonds of contract are psychologically sufficient to form stable associations). This is consistent with his legalistic understanding of his own agreement with the earlier wagon train. The natural inference from those scenes is that Tom's "not having signed anything" only slightly excuses his abandonment of the wagon train and Fen. What he owed them cannot be measured by the existence or absence of his signature on a document. At any rate, at the contracting scene in the men's bunkhouse he says, "Every man who signs on for this drive agrees to finish. There'll be no quitting

along the way; not by me and not by you." Groot is the first one
to "sign," elaborately making his mark (fig. 2.6).

IV

Dunson's perspective on this, with all its limitations and distor-
tions, is related to the deepest tension in the film. There are no
sheriffs or judges or gunfighters in this movie, so it is not a classic Western about the inauguration of the law or its psychological grip. Rather, it is about the transition between an autocratic,
charismatic, largely pre-modern or feudal form of authority to a
much more humanistic, consensus-oriented, prudent, more recognizably modern mode of rule and civil order. And this is what
constitutes the tension that we begin to see between Tom and
Matt on the drive. The dialectic is a familiar one. We can only
imagine the kind and severity of the rule or regime required in
relation to how, determinately, we imagine what lawlessness
amounts to, just what dangers it presents, and so just what needs
to be regulated (and, even more importantly, what not). And, to
return to the psychological theme, it is really often just that—an
image—that grips and guides us, as in the classic original state
of nature or original position images of Hobbes, Locke, Rousseau, Rawls, and so forth. But there is no empirical study or a
priori argument that can settle such a matter. We soon learn that
Tom clearly thinks Matt's imagination is too benign, that he is
naïve, not sufficiently aware of or motivated by the profound

2.7

consequences of even the slightest lapse from discipline and tight control. The hired gunfighter Cherry Valance (John Ireland) keeps repeating this theme for us about Matt's possible softness (fig. 2.7).[10] (The scene of each man fondling the other's gun has provoked quite a lot of discussion, too.) So half of the film's central psycho political question is expressed in Tom's worry that Matt is soft, too civilized or too feminine to rule, to be entrusted with serious political decisions.

The other half of the question is equally clear. Matt has some justifiable sense that Tom has wildly exaggerated the dangers of anarchy (as conservatives often do) and so has established an unnecessarily violent tyranny, and that his near hysteria about security and success ultimately disqualifies him from the position of ruler. More pragmatically put, Tom's means of securing order and compliance in fact destroy the order they seek to produce.

2.8

By creating tension between these two attitudes the film lets us see just what is plausible about each, making it hard to reject either out of hand. The famous stampede scene illustrates the precariousness of the situation and the dangers that Tom is worried about, why it is not wrong to be worried. The way the stampede starts is important. A cowhand, Bunk Kenneally, who has been childishly pilfering sugar the whole drive, acts again like a child, cannot keep his fingers out of the sugar, and this manifestation of immaturity starts the catastrophe and leads to the death of a well-liked cowhand. (Buck stumbles in going for the sugar and sets off a cacophony of clanging pots and pans, spooking the herd. Interestingly, the pots and pans return in the final scene [fig. 2.8].) It creates a bit of sympathy for Dunson's caution and the view that his subjects might not be mature enough for any type of rule other than his. In some ways the

2.9

stampede is a frightening image of the fragility and potential irrationality of modern mass politics (fig. 2.9).

After the stampede Tom's rule becomes much more authoritarian, even draconian. He sets out first after the man who stupidly but unintentionally started it, proposing to publicly flog him. It is clear that this unnerves everyone; by their expressions we can tell that Tom has crossed a line. A public flogging would clearly assume that Tom has some sort of public or official or legal authority, that he might even have the power to decide life or death. The tension and anxiety among the cowhands clearly stems from their confusion over this new situation. They had signed on as free agents for a commercial venture that Tom was, as "owner," to manage. But the implications of "owner" had not been clear in the contract, and they are stunned to see what Tom assumed it entailed. Bunk insists that he will not be flogged

2.10

and draws his gun. In a flash Matt outdraws him and shoots the gun out of his hand, all before Tom, who has also drawn, can shoot Bunk dead, which he admits is what he would have done. This is also the beginning of Matt's new and more fraternal leadership style—he's "one of the men" but an authority, a different sort of authority than Tom (fig. 2.10). With some contempt Tom drops the argument, telling Matt that "you shot him; you can take care of him." (Groot again assumes his persistent role in the film, staring at Tom until Tom says, "Go ahead and say it," and Groot obliges: "You was wrong, Mr. Dunson.")

The stampede destroyed the food wagon and so left the drive very low on supplies (especially coffee). This increases everyone's irritability, frustration, and impatience. The tension is heightened when they come across a wounded man who tells them he has heard there is now a rail link to Abilene, that a man named Chisolm had blazed a trail clear to Kansas. Since the man has not seen it himself, Tom discounts the testimony as hearsay and insists that they will drive on to Missouri. This prompts three of the men to say they are quitting, and in a gunfight, Matt, Tom, and Groot kill all three of them. They have backed up Tom, but they are also clearly worried. So are the men, one of whom exclaims, when Tom orders "the quitters" to be buried, and says that he will "read over them" in the morning: "Plantin' and readin', plantin' and readin'; fill a man full of lead, stick him in the ground and then read words on him. Why, when you've killed a man, why try to read the Lord in as a partner on the job?" It is the kind of question that could be asked about Tom's assumption of autocratic rule. Why, when you are a businessman on a drive, try to inflate that authority into that of a ship's commander, a general at war, or even God?

By the time of the mutiny it is easy to understand Matt's worry about Dunson's excesses. Two of his crew have "deserted," as Tom sees it, and he has not been sleeping because he is afraid more of his crew will desert. He has been drinking heavily. Wayne does an extraordinary job of conveying how much Dunson has deteriorated and aged, how close to madness he is. He was wounded in the fight with the "quitters," and that has accelerated his deterioration. Three more of the men desert in the night, and Tom sends Cherry out to bring them back. In the meantime they press on, finally recrossing the Red River itself, symbolically much more powerful at this crossing than at the first one fourteen years ago (figs. 2.11 and 2.12).

2.11

2.12

V

Matt's mutiny begins shortly thereafter. Cherry returns with two of the three men, having killed one. Tom accuses them of being "deserters" (as if this were a military enterprise) and "common thieves" (they had taken some supplies for the trail). When challenged about his legal authority to make such judgments, he says

2.13

simply and insanely, "I am the law." He reminds them that they
signed on for the whole drive, and is told, quite rightly, "I signed
the pledge, sure, but you ain't the man I signed it with." They expect to be shot by Dunson, but he shocks everyone by saying,
with a trace of a mad smile, "I'm gonna hang ya" (fig. 2.13). This
finally prompts Matt to act. He says simply, "No. No, you're not,"
and takes over the herd, with the backing of the men. They leave
Dunson and head for Abilene.

After the mutiny, when one of the "deserters" wants to grab
a gun and kill Tom, Matt physically acts out the sort of repression necessary for a new sort of rule (one which allows forgive-
ness and the reestablishment of harmony), a self-rule that
Dunson clearly is not capable of (fig. 2.14).

There are two important points about the mutiny scene.
First, viewed from a Platonic perspective Dunson is clearly a
"thymotic" man, someone whose values reflect the dominance

2.14

in his soul not of desire and appetite (he is shown to reject the pull of the erotic, and he is not driven by appetite, clearly seeing himself more as an emperor than as a businessman) or of reason (he is impulsive, seeks no compromise, and is often, by the standards of prudence, clearly "wrong") but of thymos, spiritedness, the will to achieve distinction and status, to be and to be known to be the doer of great deeds, subject to rage when he feels slighted or disrespected. Hence the emphasis on his branding everything he owns. But such a man thrives only in a particular context. When that context begins to change (when the world becomes, as Hegel says, prosaic, not heroic), he can look more and more like a psychotic (the way he says "I'm gonna hang ya" clearly betrays the beginnings of madness) or at least an anachronism. It is time for the more prudent and much more fraternal and egalitarian Matt to take over.

Second, we return to the issue of contracts and promises, to how one can bind one's future self by a present agreement. This is a crucial issue in the American context because of the challenge to the notion posed by secession. In this scene the cowhands in effect make the South's argument, and it is not easy to dismiss it. To the claim that they promised not to leave, they understandably respond, "Yes, but you ain't the man I signed it with." One can hear the echo of the southern claim: "Yes, we made a covenant to form a union, but the union we formed was a slaveholding union. Indeed, that institution was inscribed in our founding document, the Constitution." "This 1860 union ain't," in effect, "the union we formed by covenant." In both mutiny and secession we can see the relative uselessness of the appeal to "what one contracted to do" and the greater importance of authority, power, and the right understanding of human psychology in sustaining such a contract.

VI

The narrative frame of the movie as it continues is somewhat cyclical, reinforcing by repetition the differences (at least the surface differences) between Matt's rule and Dunson's. After Matt takes over the herd, and advance scouts come back to report that there is a wagon train ahead of them with coffee and women (coffee being clearly the priority), Matt's fraternal rule is clear. He knows "what the men need" and is not obsessed with using every spare second on the drive, and he indulges rather than denies himself and the men. (He is one of them, not really a "ruler." This silently raises the question of what Matt would have done had he been in Dunson's place when men started to defect, gravely threatening the rest of them.) He takes a break, even has time for a very hastily set-up romance with Tess (who is shot with an arrow—an Indian's, not Cupid's, but the somewhat clumsy point is made.)[11] Moreover, when Matt sees the wagon train under attack he risks a great deal to help drive off the Indians, and the contrast with Dunson's abandonment of his wagon train and his beloved is clear. (Matt seems to be both redeeming what Tom was "wrong" about and repeating what Tom did. He also does not take his beloved Tess with him, saying, we learn from her later, that she was "not strong enough," that he had work to do that a woman could not help with.)

The chance encounter with the endangered wagon train sets up one of the oddest sequences in the film. After Matt and the herd have left, Dunson and his hired crew appear, and Tess takes care of Tom and talks with him about Matt. In a bizarre offer, Tom promises her half of all he owns if she will bear him a son. The episode has a strange intimacy and knowingness about it. Tom does not, we learn from his reactions later, really expect her to accept his offer; it seems more in the way of a "test," a way of finding out if she loves Matt or is a fortune hunter. (She is after all with a troop of what look like gamblers,

2.15

show people, and perhaps prostitutes.) Tom keeps avowing that he will kill Matt, but there is something in his affect that makes his promises unbelievable. He acts more like a rejected lover by exaggerating what he will do to the beloved, and, in this case, reliving his own error with Fen, a mistake that has colored his whole life. The long conversation scene seems like an afterthought, but it helps to explain a great deal in the film's dénouement.

At any rate, Matt and the boys successfully bring the herd to Abilene; there *is* a rail link, so these venture capitalists with their sweat equity have won. But Dunson reappears for the climactic scene, an extraordinary "visual" as he strides through the cattle, intent on killing his adopted son (fig. 2.15).

Cherry tries to intervene but is wounded by Tom. When Tom advances on Matt, Matt does not react; he is passive, with a serene smile on his face. But they fight brutally until it is ended

2.16

by Tess, who fires a gun and declares that "any fool with half a mind can see that you two love each other" (fig. 2.16).

VII

This ending has been much criticized as a typical Hollywood Happy Ending that betrays the violence and passion of the rest of the movie. And it is true that Joanne Dru's speech is corny and the buddy scene at the end a bit kitschy, and that the transition of Dunson from anger incarnate, all Achilles all the time, to sweetness and light, happily yielding to Matt ("I'm not going to tell you what to do"), is breathtaking in its rapidity.[12] (Hawks himself in an interview said that after having made Dunson lose everything of importance to him, his beloved especially, he did not have the heart to kill him off.)[13] But the fact that there is no fight to the death is interesting in itself, and I would like to conclude with a somewhat heterodox defense of such a claim.

For one thing, it suggests that this transition of power from Dunson to Matt *is not inherently revolutionary*. It does not require an eruption of violence and death. Instead, it is depicted as internally necessary; it is a more organic and natural transition if indeed it is a transition at all. It is also interesting that such a view (that the stakes *are* such that only violence can decide whose view of the conditions of rule is correct) is Dunson's and that Matt refuses to fight, to buy into such a scenario. (The film's point of view on this point as on so many others seems to be Matt's.) He expresses a kind of weird confidence as he allows himself to be shot at and pummeled, as if, to stretch the point, he knows he has "history" on his side. (One could also say that Matt embodies the antiheroic, prosaic world of bourgeois modernity, where authority and power have to be distributed to be effective, where the fate of the community cannot hang on the actions of one hero.)[14] We begin to suspect that the core of the Dunson problem has much more to do with Dunson's self-mythologization, his *fantasy* about rule, empire, independence, and strength of will, something I have suggested is a deeply American fantasy. (His passions are not merely somatic reactions; his distaste with any, even erotic, dependence, and so his pride and accompanying anger, make sense not only in a historical world of a certain shape, but such a world is itself an imagined world, and the grip of such an imagined picture has its own historical location as well.)

But Matt ultimately must defend himself, and he begins to fight back, prompting Groot to express relief that "it's gonna be alright." He too was apparently afraid that Matt might be unable to stand up to the tyrannical Dunson, either because he was weak or because he loved Dunson too much, or both. (The "Schmittean" question of whether bourgeois, liberal, commercial republics and their avatars like Matt can foster the psychological qualities necessary for order and self-defense—how to think about the relation between commercial mass societies and the psychology necessary for politics—will play a large role in the next Western we look at.) The key line about the relevant psychological issue is spoken by Joanne Dru, as this tension between patriarchy and fraternal rule is momentarily and completely unexpectedly trumped by matriarchal power. She says that "any fool with half a mind can see that you two love each other."

This is extraordinary for two reasons. It sums up her frustration and perhaps ours (what Hawks knew would be ours) that the great struggle over the fate and direction of the herd, the struggle for power and supremacy that we have been watching with something like Groot's anxiety, *has* been a kind of shadow play, an illusion, or, as I have been suggesting, a fantasy largely staged by Dunson to justify himself. There never was any great struggle, never any real threat of a fight to the death. (In the conversation with Tess at the camp, Dunson seems to know this already.) To say all at once the point I am trying to make: The mythic struggle we have been watching is itself the result of a kind of self-mythologization (exactly like the *Tales of Early Texas* myth "inside" the film's own mythic narration), a fantasy narrative frame that is also demythologizing itself in front of us.

There is a deep connection, I am suggesting, between the elaborate play on point of view and perspective staged at the opening and throughout the intertitles and the substance of the story. As viewers, we tend to buy into the epic-heroic self-presentation of the narrative; a great but flawed, Lear-like man is attempting a great thing of momentous importance for the nation, even as the success in that enterprise will render him irrelevant. But the civic and political dimensions of the story seem firmly rooted only in fantasy; the reality we actually see is private and erotic.

It nevertheless remains a dangerous and violent fantasy, and we should not underestimate its hold on the human imagination. This revelation does nothing to account for the Indians and Mexicans whom Dunson has killed in his claim to possess the land. And we need to note that the "love" Tess speaks of, while it makes clear that the transition to Matt's humanism is supposed to be seamless and "natural," it is also thoroughly male and artificial (based on the exclusion of women, both mothers and lovers) and thereby somewhat pathological. Matt is just securing more solidly the possession of and rule over a vast cattle empire created by theft and killing.[15]

Second, Tess's frustration that she has worried for naught, that there really was no great struggle between these two and what they stand for, also means that not much of a "transition" has occurred. Or rather, that the transition is a strategic one, that Matt does not really threaten Dunson, he just represents a more efficient, reliable way to preserve what Dunson stands for. Matt, it turns out, *is* Dunson's true son if not biological heir. (They often smoke the same cigarette; Matt has picked up Dunson's affectation of rubbing his finger on the side of his nose.) I suggest that this is disturbing (dramatically and for what it says about the American imaginary), not redemptive or progressive, and that this is what is bothersome about the ending, not its dramatic limitations. Dunson, with his extreme sense of entitlement, his monomania and rage, his rejection of love and romance (as "soft" and feminine), his brutality and self-mythologization, is a hard man to love, and the political vision he represents is shown to be based on a self-serving exaggeration of the dangers of lawlessness and a corresponding inflation of his importance.[16] Matt's gamble, it turns out, was that Dunson's purposes could be better achieved by some measure of civil trust in testimony, something essential to a commercial republic, and by indulging the crew rather than terrorizing them by autocratic rule and Spartan discipline.[17] Since the film is actually about financial speculation, risk taking, and the new world of commerce, one could easily make the case that Matt's decision to try for Abilene is actually the "tough" one. There was real uncertainty over whether there *was* a railroad in Abilene, and, as we see later, there was an even more pressing question in Abilene: whether anyone with any cattle would show up! (In general, the view of commercial republics in the film is pacific—the Adam Smith view of the virtues of a commercial society, not the Ayn Rand view of competitive struggle. The genial cattle buyer at the end of the film is genial for a reason. He will match or better any price Matt can find because he wants Matt as a future customer.

So the great psychological question everyone was worried about—"Is Matt tough enough?"—never is answered, for it was the wrong question posed in the wrong terms. It is extremely important, I think, that all Matt does in the mutiny scene is talk. In a remarkable demonstration of the "distributed" and so nonheroic but very effective character of bourgeois subjectivity, it is Cherry who injures Dunson's hand and Buster (Noah Berry Jr.'s character) who shoots away Dunson's gun, and it is not Matt who ends or resolves his fight with Dunson but a woman who invokes love while firing a pistol, a woman who in this scene seems more a mother to squabbling children than a future wife. Matt simply represents the modern, equally but differently tough side of Dunson, not his alternative. He shares the rule but remains the "one who decides to share it" and so retains power, even if a new form of power.

But this issue opens up onto countless others. The interplay between Tom and Matt invokes countless mythic themes. I haven't had time to discuss an obvious one: that Tom embodies an Old Testament severity and anger in his sense of strict righteousness and judgmental wrath, and Matt is very "New Testament," especially in that striking scene of his Christ-like willingness to turn the other cheek (which is promptly shot), his extraordinary confidence that this display of his "nonviolence" will not lead to him getting killed. Of course he fights eventually, but only as a last resort, and in a way that is rightly characterized by Tess as not serious, as if inspired by a confidence that the love between him and Tom will triumph over their struggle. When framed in this way, the complex and oddly Foucauldean question raised by Tess's remarks—How much of a revolution *is* the shift from the exercise of external coercive authority to a more humanistic cooption of opposition and rebellion (to a more complex form of self-discipline)?—is worthy of a much longer discussion.[18]

So it is significant that at the very end both Tom and Matt tumble theatrically into the clanging trappings of the bourgeois domestic world (fig. 2.17). They crash into that cart of kitchen implements, pots and pans, colanders, bolts of cloth, an unheroic world that from their perspective might seem to be the feminine world but one which is inevitable, which is "all around them." The scene also harks back to the clanging cascade of pots and pans that incited the stampede. They are no longer in the precivilized world and subject to such danger (so goes the "picture" anyway) but are literally covered with the

2.17

trappings of peaceful domesticity. It is not a particularly heroic picture.[19]

This image could sum up a conventional view of where we are left: that the era of heroes is over, no longer necessary in the world of bankers, beef buyers, and railroads; or it could suggest that we are being reminded that that bourgeois world is itself a world of civilized and hidden ruthlessness, more efficient and more "humane" profiteering from the original seizure and colonization of Indian and Mexican land. I don't think there is any resolution in the film, and the vague unease we are left with is one of the film's great achievements.

But this image is not the last one. That is reserved for a single image that says all at once and eloquently that the "transition" to civilized order and the rule of law that so many Westerns present is not as substantial a transition as we would like to

2.18

think. What we think we left behind is actually still present and deeply linked to what on the surface seems a much more humane, egalitarian order. Here is the film's ending, Dunson drawing a picture of the new brand, with both his and Matt's initials equally prominent (fig. 2.18).[20]

3 WHO CARES WHO SHOT LIBERTY VALANCE?

The Heroic and the Prosaic in *The Man Who Shot Liberty Valance*

I

HUMAN beings make myths, tell stories about ancient times and great events, and call such times and events to mind over many generations, for all sorts of reasons. But many of these reasons are political. They help confirm a people's identity and help legitimate entitlements to territory and authority; they might orient a people with a sense of their unique mission.[1] They attempt to master the brute contingency of history by making some sense out of events, pointing to patterns and unities and resolutions; they attempt to domesticate, make familiar, the strangeness of the world and the place of human beings in it. People tell political stories of origins, foundings, liberation, unification or lost unity, heroic resistance, martyrdom, redemption, privileged election, and so forth. The way that mythic accounts achieve such functions involves those aspects of human psychology relevant to politics; it requires that we understand political psychology.

The United States is a very young country by world or mythic standards, and so our ancient times are not very ancient. But one of our mythic forms of self-understanding, I have claimed (along with several others), could be said to be the very best Hollywood Westerns. They deal with a past form of life that is self-consciously treated as gone, unrecoverable (even if still quite powerfully and somewhat mysteriously attractive) and, while not very ancient, as contributions to the American imaginary many tell a basic and clearly troubling, complicated story of a traumatic, decisive political transition, the end of one sort of order and self-image and the beginning of another. They represent a kind of myth of American modernization.[2]

This modernization theme is an extremely important one in our national character. For America does not have a very long historical tradition and very little common ethnic and cultural heritage. Knowing that someone is an American and just that, you usually know a good deal less about him or her than if you knew he or she were Chinese or Ukranian, from countries with ancient, territorially based communities, and even something less than you would know about other immigrant societies, such as Canada or New Zealand. As Michael Walzer has put it, no one in America speaks of the fatherland or the motherland or of a common *patrie*. And, again as he puts it, the republican ideal of vigorous public citizenship was overtaken in the nineteenth century by a liberal ideal of rights protection, a rather thin citizenship, and a vigorous, pluralistic civil society of voluntary associations.[3] The United States has been said by Horace Kallen in the 1920s to be a "political nation of cultural nationalities,"[4] and by John Rawls a "social union of social unions,"[5] and that in itself raises the question of what sort of political nation this could be. Voluntary associations of all sorts take up a good deal more of the public energy of Americans than in other countries, and the nature and robustness of American citizenship has been debated for a long time. It is famously a mobile, fast-moving, and, after the nineteenth century especially, polyglot place, often inattentive to its own brief history, even in popular art forms. Its greatest historical event was that it once fell apart in a brutal, long, fratricidal civil war, and it sometimes can seem as if it never put itself back together again. However, just because of that, the ideal of modernity, both in the official European Enlightenment sense (the authority of reason, science, tolerance, a faith in the social good of technology and unregulated markets) and in the general cultural sense of a progressive, ever-improving people, is central—probably more than any other element—to what makes Americans who they are. In one sense, becoming an American is easy; you commit yourself to the principles of a regime, in this case to paradigmatically modern principles.[6] On the other hand, just what the implications of such a commitment are can be quite murky. Being an American is essentially a *political* identification (political ideals are all that hold us together as a nation), but what is the content, especially the psychological content, of such an identification? What counts psychologically as such a commitment? We approach again the question raised in the last chapter: Is there much of a psychological reality to political self-identification in America, and if not, is that a worrisome problem or not?[7]

II

Again, a scene from a Western can demonstrate how complicated this can be. In the famous closing scene of Fred Zinnemann's controversial, gripping drama *High Noon*, Marshal Kane (Gary Cooper) has been saved from an almost certain death, but the townspeople had refused to help him fight off the killers who have come for revenge against Kane, the agent of the law that imprisoned them. They will cooperate in their religious and civic associations (their most dramatic refusal of the duties of citizenship occurs in a church, and the convincing argument not to help concerns the economic disadvantages of any gun-fight on their streets), but they will risk nothing when called on as citizens. Kane has been saved by his wife, Amy (Grace Kelly), a near-fanatically committed Quaker who finally breaks with the code of nonviolence, shoots one killer in the back, and helps Kane kill the last one. Zinnemann wants us to see that it is the civil institution of marriage that turned out to have real authority, to inspire genuine allegiance, *not* any political bond. (Hence the brilliant contrasting shot of Amy's wedding band as she

3.1

embraces Kane, and Kane's tin star as the camera shifts to a frontal view.) The question of whether there *is* any true political life in the emerging America is answered here by Kane's famous contemptuous gesture with that badge of office, the symbolic counterpart to the ring. He tosses it to the dust in a gesture of obvious contempt (fig. 3.1).

If the question is how it is possible to form a national political unity, especially without a common long tradition on the same territory, and more specifically, given the way people are so strongly pulled toward concern with their own, the local and private, if the question is how such distinctly political attachment is psychologically possible, the bleak answer represented by that gesture is: in the United States, it likely won't ever be possible, and the consequences are quite worrisome. Indeed, what is represented as happening in *High Noon* does not even yet point to our own cultural and ethnic divisions (which make the problem much worse) but to the simple absence of any feeling of a common stake in taking a stand against the killers.[8]

(Great Westerns being what they are, the ending also manages to create a lot of questions. In some sense the townspeople are right; if Kane leaves, Frank Miller and his men will not bother the town. He is no longer sheriff, so not their problem. His taking a stand can be understood as flowing from his sense of duty, a kind of "my station, my duties" attitude, and so as evidence that his fate and the town's are linked, but it can also look like the expression of what was for Rousseau and Hobbes the most dangerous pre-modern passion: vanity or vainglory or amour propre. Cooper's anxious, hesitant, imploring performance does not seem to me to support such a reading, however.)

Of course myths, whether epic or romantic or, as in the *High Noon* case, tragic, a story of a failed founding, are not arguments in defense of anything; nor are they premises in some claim about the best way to live. So they are raising questions about a certain way of life and affirming some way or rejecting others in ways that are not traditional topics in either political philosophy or political science. I have suggested that they are raising questions about political psychology in a form that requires a great deal of interpretative and evaluative work to get at and think about. In Howard Hawks's *Red River* emotions are engaged among the characters, passions enflamed, fears excited in a manner that can be understood only if we understand something of the epic self-consciousness imagined and projected by the charismatic main character, his take on what they are doing, and the ultimate inappropriateness of this epic mode of self-understanding at the beginning of what would be a modern market economy. One of the interesting things about the film is that it manages to suggest both something troubling *and* heroic about Tom Dunson's self-mythologization, even as it portrays the inevitable, genuinely progressive but somehow also vaguely unsatisfying or dispiriting, less stirring or charismatic "rule" of characters like Matt Garth.

III

This is a large theme indeed. It reminds us immediately that another obvious way to understand the relevance of political psychology to modern political life is to consider the kinds of criticisms made of liberal-democratic commercial republics by so many prominent European political philosophers. Rousseau's account of modern society, for example, depends heavily on a theory about the right relation between desires and capacities, the artificial origin of human vanity, and our state of psychological dependence. So from the end of the *Second Discourse:* "The savage lives in himself; sociable man always outside himself, is capable of living only in the opinions of others and, so to speak, derives the sentiment of his own existence only from their judgment."[9]

What kind of criticism is this, that sociable, modern man lives "outside himself," and why is it a criticism relevant to politics? (And whatever this question is, as a general worry about a distinctive modern form of conformism and corrupting social dependence, it is not Rousseau's alone. It resurfaces in Tocqueville, Emerson, Nietzsche, Mill, Arendt, and others.)

Or consider how Hegel described the modern world in an early work: as fragmented, disunified (suffering from "dividedness, *Entzweiung*, or even "torn apartness," *Zerissenheit*). Or Marx's complaint that in capitalism the worker experiences the product of his labor as an "alien object" or that he is alienated, "strange to" other human beings, or that in capitalism commodities are experienced in an objectionable way, "fetishized." Or Nietzsche's complaint that what is wrong with modern Christian humanism is that it is born out of weakness, self-hatred, and resentment against the strong, is a "herd morality," and so will ultimately prove to be poisonous, psychologically unhealthy. Or Weber's famous complaint that living in bureaucratic modernity was like living in an "iron cage," that we were producing "specialists without spirit, sensualists without heart," and that "this nullity imagines that it has obtained a level of civilization never before achieved."[10] (His even bleaker characterization of this: "the polar night of icy darkness.")[11] Or Heidegger's dramatic pronouncement that modernity was the age of nihilism and profound thoughtlessness, the "age of consummate meaninglessness." Or, in effect, Carl

Schmitt's elaborate version of the old joke that a liberal is a person who cannot take his own side in an argument, that bourgeois liberal democracies are so oriented to debate and compromise that they will not be able to muster the collective will necessary to defend themselves from their true enemies. Or Leo Strauss's worry that even our basic experience of good and evil, noble and base, might become lost and forgotten in the confusing pulls and pushes of modern egalitarianism.

As long as we do not think of psychology as exclusively "whatever is now studied by research psychologists," we can clearly recognize that the heart of these attacks is that modern political life—rights-based, egalitarian regimes committed above all to prosperity and peace—is psychologically unsatisfying or even psychologically unworthy of human beings. This is not a worry, in other words, raised about what people believe. It does not have directly to do with false beliefs, superstition, or mistaken reasoning, and so whatever problems are being noted, they are not correctable simply by "enlightenment." (Perhaps that is one of the reasons many would prefer not to raise them. Short of paternalistic and scary reeducation programs, it is not at all clear what do about them, ever the first American question, especially by students.)

This is not to say that we are irrational or passion-driven machines. How we end up thinking about, evaluating, and reflecting on the meaning of the various passions that are experienced as

inclining us powerfully to do or forebear from doing various
things is obviously also of crucial importance. Our views shape
the way our experiences are actually felt and help us imagine
means to realize what we decide we ought to do. This just means
that the psychological picture is quite complicated.

Moreover, it would not be very intelligent, I think, to insist
that the concerns registered above really involve "social issues
and social philosophy," do not touch the problem of political
authority. The whole point of many of these criticisms is to
counter such a pedantic separation, to argue that political judgments, expressions, allegiances, and activities necessarily reflect ideals, commitments, and fears already formed in social
life, that is, in religious, economic, and cultural life, and so that
the very possibility of politics cannot be properly understood
without understanding how social concerns are either expressed
in politics or are such that they prevent the activity of genuine
politics from emerging. (One thinks again, for example, of
Arendt.)[12] It was certainly clear to the originators of the modern notion of contractual secular political authority that mere
acknowledgment of the rationality of political contract was
insufficient to account either for the mythical founding act itself or for the sustained allegiance, sacrifice, and civic cooperation necessary for a state to be and to survive as a state. The
fear of violent death, the powerful desire for a commodious
and prosperous life, a natural sociability, and many other can-
didates for the role of decisive political passion entered the

discussion and, as one astute commentator put it, the "crisis of allegiance" in seventeenth-century thought and experience was in effect "inseparable from what we might call a crisis of the affections."[13]

IV

There are two contrasting scenes from John Ford's 1962 film, his last work of genius, *The Man Who Shot Liberty Valance*, that frame the most ambitious theme in the movie and which begin to raise the topics just discussed.[14] The setting is the town of Shinbone, somewhere in a wild western state not otherwise identified.[15] The first is a scene from the major narration in the film, which is, just to complicate things, a flashback, the tale told by one of the main protagonists, Ransom "Ranse" Stoddard (James Stewart). (And, we should remember, a tale told by a successful politician to a group of journalists. More on that later.)[16] This is, let us say, the pre–law and order Shinbone, from the perspective of the film's time, long ago. We see a very crowded, very noisy, boisterous saloon. (And if we didn't get the visual point, the band is playing "There'll Be a Hot Time in the Old Town Tonight.") A drunk is tossed out the front door, to the raucous laughter of several apparently respectable town women. We see that there are many Mexicans in the town, and a Mexican place of business next to the saloon (fig. 3.2). Shinbone is rowdy but obviously a bustling place, full of life if also danger.

3.2

The contrasting scene is the official beginning of the movie, set in the historical present. (All three movies begin in a similar way, with motion coming right at the viewer: a wagon train, a railroad engine, and a lone horseman, almost as if out of the past and at the present. All three also, by the way, involve the John Wayne character giving up, withdrawing from, or denying himself a relationship with a woman [figs. 3.3 and 3.4].)

Everything in contemporary Shinbone is clean, very brightly lit, extraordinarily orderly, and, in a way, oddly still, almost dead, especially by comparison with earlier Shinbone. (There is an aura of death, of course, because a man, an old friend, has died. But the age of the Stoddards, wife Hallie's melancholy, and the contrast between the nearly still modern Shinbone and the premodern Shinbone suggest a more pervasive and mysterious aura.)[17] We see only a few citizens, and everything is quiet. (The presence of Mexicans had been so prominently foregrounded

3.3

3.4

that it is noticeable that none are to be seen in the new Shinbone.) Ranse has become a very important man, and he has
learned to talk like such a man trying to sound humble. He
sounds more than a tad pompous here and in the final scenes,
though. He is now a successful and powerful politician (not one

of Ford's favorite character types) and acting the part as it needs
to be acted. (Indeed, he is what is often referred to by type as
the great American success story: from dishwasher to governor
to senator and ambassador.) The efficiency and orderliness of
everything is stressed. Ranse compliments the conductor for
the punctuality of the train, and we see that old Shinbone even
has telephones now. But his demeanor does set a stark contrast
with that of his wife, whom we will come to know as a brave,
lively, spirited woman. She is understandably in mourning for
an old friend, but something more melancholic and somewhat
mysterious seems to be going on. In some ways she looks like a
broken, defeated, ghostly person.

As the film opens, the local press is intrigued that a famous
person would come to their little town because of the death of
someone no one has heard of. (Tom has been forgotten, and we
realize that there is no indication that Ransom or Hallie has
ever been in touch with their old friend.) The journalists de-
mand the story with surprising stridency as the "public's right."
Stoddard in effect gets permission from Hallie to talk with the
journalists. (What is quite crucially unclear and what remains
unclear is whether she has thereby given him permission to tell
the true story of the beginning of his career in politics and the
crucial role played by Tom Doniphon. It is never clear whether
she even knows the true story.)[18] Hallie goes to Tom's ranch (the
visit seems like a stop at ancient ruins) and gets a cactus rose for
Tom's coffin.

As Ranse begins his story we learn of his arrival in Shin-bone as a young man, and we see his stagecoach robbed and an enraged Liberty Valance (Lee Marvin in his finest role)[19] toss around Stoddard's law books with contempt and administer a horrible beating with a whip. Tom Doniphon finds Ranse and brings him back to Hallie's restaurant, where her parents, the Ericsons, agree to nurse Ranse back to health. (In another con-trast here with the modern Shinbone, the old, lawless place was also a place of mutual aid, unhesitatingly responsive to the needs of others in an open acknowledgment of human dependence. Modern Shinbone is a colder place, and the main social relation we see is commercial; the newspapermen want something from Stoddard so they can sell newspapers.) Ranse insists on work-ing at the Ericson restaurant as a dishwasher to pay off his debt to them. This means that, in the view of the town, he is femi-nized, wearing an apron and waiting on tables.[20] Valance comes in one night and calls him the "new waitress." He trips Stod-dard, who is carrying a plate, and is about to humiliate him further when Tom intervenes, saying that it was his steak that had been dropped and insisting that Valance pick it up. Stod-dard cannot believe what he is seeing, that two men are in a fight to the death over a slab of meat, and *he* picks it up. (As a repre-sentative of the new bourgeois order, in other words, he is aston-ished at what an honor code, or the pre-modern cult of pride, requires. It seems to him childish and bizarre, although, as we shall see, he will be drawn into it somewhat.)

These initial scenes raise a question and point to the obvious plot development. Valance has been hired by the large cattle ranchers "north of the picket wire river" (the free range anti-fence people who are the ubiquitous villains in so many Westerns) to terrorize the smaller farmers and ranchers and so to prevent statehood and the regulation and supervision that comes with it. This sets up the mythic, archetypal, familiar setting for our new founding. Tom is one of these small ranchers, and it is established that he is the only one around good enough with a gun to face down and end Valance's reign of terror. He is willing to kill Valance over a dropped steak; so why not fight for the common good, especially since he has a stake (no pun intended) in it, a small horse ranch?

We get some indication later that it is precisely *because* he feels so self-sufficient and independent that he sees no need for adopting a civic role. He is confident that he can defend himself and his land, and he worries that if there is a move to statehood it will increase the level of violence and intrude on his private plans for a ranch with Hallie. There is a brief indication of how he views the situation in a scene when he returns to Shinbone and interrupts the lesson at a small schoolhouse Ranse has set up. He insists that the local newspaper editor Peabody's honest journalism and the agitation for statehood will create chaos; that these well-intentioned people are starting something they will not be able to finish. And later, when he declines a nomination for the state convention, he says, "'Cause I got plans, personal plans."

It does not seem to have occurred to him that the benefits of literacy and a civic life might be worth some risk, even a great risk (on the contrary, he is shown as personally halting the progress toward literacy, sending the children home, and as cruelly indifferent to hired hand Pompey's aspirations in this scene, the only one where he treats Pompey with something a good deal less than respect). Moreover, he is wrong. The cattle barons do not succeed, or, somewhat surprisingly, even come close to succeeding, in disrupting the territorial convention. Blood does not run in the streets of Shinbone. We are presumably meant to appreciate that the euphoria and common-mindedness forged by Ranse's killing Liberty Valance has created a solidarity and strength that was unanticipated in Tom's warnings.

The plot then turns on romance. We see that Tom has for some time intended to marry Hallie and bring her out to the small ranch he is building and enlarging for that purpose. But we also see that Hallie is immediately drawn to the educated and cultivated, and yet also extremely brave (if unskilled) and somewhat patronizing Ranse Stoddard. And when we learn that Ranse will begin to teach her how to read and write, and promises some day to show her a "real rose" (as if cactus roses were not real), we know where all this is headed and what awaits poor Tom.

Although it would lead far into another discussion, we need also to note briefly, as further testimony to the complexity of the film, that Ford does not leave Tom's assertion of self-sufficiency uncommented upon. Tom never seems to properly acknowledge how vital to his security and protection is his black defender, (his "boy") Pompey. His sense of his own grand, almost divine self-sufficiency is obviously blind to this aspect of his and all human dependence. Ford clearly also wants us to see this blindness as a figure for American collective blindness to this dependence and hence this debt to African-Americans. In the schoolhouse scene Pompey is denied by Tom the chance to learn much about even the myth of American egalitarianism, and it is understandable that he cannot quite remember that the slaveholding Thomas Jefferson states, in the Declaration of Independence, that "all men are created equal." In a brilliant line reading, Woody Strode, after a pregnant pause, admits, "I knew that Mr. Ranse, but I just plumb forgot it."

V

But now, however, we can go no further without reminding ourselves that this is *Stoddard's* narration, and there are signs that this fact might be coloring what we are seeing. Valance is evil to the point of raving psychosis, a malevolent force more than a human being, a possible exaggeration that would help rationalize Stoddard's actions. We never have a scene of Tom and Hallie alone, and only occasionally and incidentally do we see indications of what must have been true: that Hallie has given and continues to give Tom indications that she loves him too. The marshal, Link Appleyard, whom we meet in the movie's present, is hardly the grossly incompetent buffoon we meet in Ranse's narration. Age could have given him more dignity, of course, but the contrast seems too striking for that explanation alone. The characterization (Ranse's characterization) of the dignified Pompey portrays him as occasionally very servile, in a way suspiciously consistent with Ranse's crude attempt to give him cash in the final scenes, calling it "pork chop money." And most strangely, there is almost nothing remotely romantic and certainly nothing at all erotic in the relationship between Hallie and Ranse. The only scenes of tenderness are maternal, the two times Hallie must dress Ranse's wounds. At all other points the "love" between them, such as it is, is expressed (that is, *Stoddard* expresses it) as Hallie looking up in awe at the cultivated lawyer. He "wins" Hallie without ever really asking for her.[21] Put another way, what Hallie is choosing in Ranse is not so much him as what he represents, a life much different from that of a cafe owner's daughter or even the wife of a small-town lawyer.

VI

As matters develop, Valance calls out Stoddard for a final duel, and Ranse decides to face Valance in the street, armed with a pathetic ancient handgun.[22] Hallie knows Ranse will be killed and begs Tom to help. This is not a happy choice for Tom—if Stoddard dies in the duel, he will have Hallie all to himself; if he saves Ranse, Hallie is lost to him. Nevertheless, he does help. (Tom is chivalrous to a fault; he is a much more sexual presence than Ranse but also considerably more courtly and attentive to Hallie than Ranse, who seems most interested in teaching her.)[23] In a complex triangulated action, just as Ranse is about to be killed by Valance, and as Ranse is about to fire an ineffective shot back, Tom fires at exactly the same moment, killing Valance. That is, unseen, he shoots him down from a dark corner, violating every code of the West. ("Cold-blooded murder. But I can live with it. Hallie's happy.") (figs. 3.5 and 3.6).

What this suggests is that the conditions necessary for law and political order are doubly morally problematic. First, there can be no law unless the lawless are eliminated, controlled,

3.5

3.6

but given what the lawless are willing to do, this violent elimi-
nation cannot itself be just or fair, cannot play by the rules.
Valance is *ambushed*, shot down from the dark. Second, it
seems that a civilized order must view itself as founded by heroic and unproblematic violence, so this truth about the founding must be hidden by a lie. Apparently a victory over Liberty
Valance (over unconstrained "liberty" as an absolute "value")
by Tom Doniphon would just be one more episode in a cycle of
violence, revenge, and intimidation.[24] Valance must be killed
by a representative of a new order; his death must *mean* that.
So since Tom is unseen and quickly vanishes, everybody can
think that Ransom Stoddard killed Valance and so can dis-
tinguish this act of violence from a personal one by associating
it with Ranse's ideals, can believe that the rule of law and democracy triumphed. Violence before there is law is unavoidably

3.7

lawless, but if it is for the sake of law the paradox can be less-
ened if not eliminated.[25]

Tom returns to his house and in a fury about his lost future
burns down half of it and almost himself (fig. 3.7). This scene
is poignant in all sorts of ways. It reveals how desperately Tom
wanted to escape the warrior life of the self-sufficient cowboy
(a persistent theme in ex-gunfighter movies too, like *Shane* and
Man of the West). Here Tom wants, it appears, both to return to, to
crawl inside, a home figuring as a kind of womb, what would have
been the birthplace of a new life, and burn up inside it, consuming
it and himself with his own passion. It is instructive that he is
saved by Pompey, the only dependable erotic link with the world
that he will ever have.[26] It is also a nice touch that Tom is laid out
in the buckboard just as Liberty Valance was (and just as Ranse
was when he was brought into Shinbone). Their fates are linked.

Ranse Stoddard becomes the Man Who Shot Liberty Valance, and we are plunged into the thick of the question of the role of mythology, or more prosaically in this context, untruth and fantasy, in the creation of a political world and in its psychological "health."

When Ranse is about to be chosen a delegate to the state convention though, he demurs, sickened by the fact that he is popular because he killed a man, upset that his precious law requires such violent extralegal means. It is at this point that Tom draws him aside and tells him, contemptuously, "You didn't kill Liberty Valance," and relates the truth in his own flashback. He then tells Ranse that since he has taught Hallie to read, he now must give her something to read about. He must go into politics and succeed, and Tom knows that this means he, Tom, will have lost Hallie forever.

Tom prefaces the story with quite an elaborate puff of cigarette smoke, as if to suggest that the meaning of what we are about to see is going to be hard to fathom. And of course there is always the distinct possibility that (a) Tom is fabricating everything—perhaps he just stood by in the alley and watched Ranse get off a lucky shot, or (b) now that Tom is dead, Ranse wants to shift what he knows is his own responsibility for killing Valance to Tom, perhaps in order that his (Ranse's own) "legend" will not revolve around a murder. At any rate, the smoke is a very pronounced piece of stage business that Ford has set up

3.8

in order to return to it in the film's closing scene, as Ranse begins to light his pipe (fig. 3.8).

We also need to think about why Tom's revelation changed
Ranse's mind about running for office. He *was* worried about the
extralegal and amoral violence necessary to jump-start politics in
Shinbone. Once he learns that the moral situation is even worse
than he imagined (that Valance was "murdered in cold blood"),
but that at least *he* hadn't shot anybody, he is willing to be a delegate to the statehood convention. How should we explain this?
Is it his appreciation of the magnitude of Tom's sacrifice? The
mere fact that he, Ranse, is "technically" innocent of wrongdoing?
A more sober and pragmatic realization of the necessity of these
moral compromises? An acceptance of Tom's argument that since
Ranse has led Hallie to believe that a real transition from the
state of brute self-interest and violence is possible, he now must
carry through and actually make it a reality?

We return then to real time, the old Ranse with the journalists. Then a number of stunning events occur. Ranse has finally told the truth about who killed Liberty Valance, but the newspaper editor, Maxwell Scott, refuses to print it. He sacrifices quite a story, and one can imagine the banner headlines in today's press: "Man Who Shot Liberty Valance Revealed as Fraud," "Hero's Life Based on Lie," and so forth.

But Scott justifies his actions by saying, "When the legend becomes fact, print the legend." He could have said, "This is the West. We need our heroes and legends. It will serve no purpose now to destroy this useful legend. I don't think we'll print the true story," etc. What he says is much more extreme and enigmatic. Then there is the added complication that the film we have just seen has shown *us* that a community's self-mythologizing is based on an untruth.[27] (The same paradoxical ending famously occurs in *Fort Apache*, although it is much more morally problematic there.)[28] Does this mean that *we* no longer need legends?[29] It is impossible to say to oneself: I know these legendary accounts are false, but we need to treat them as facts, so I will.[30] You can't make yourself believe something because you think it is good that you so believe. So the film has just disconnected legend and fact for us, although the editor tries to justify withholding the truth from his readers.

The train arrives and the Stoddards must leave. We then learn a very great deal in a very few compressed minutes about the relationship between Ranse and Hallie over all these years that backshadows a bit what we just seen and probably assumed and that raises in a new way several questions about Ranse and his founding act (or nonaction). (There is also something *missing* from the final scenes that says as much as any dialogue. Ford, without any comment or highlight of the fact in the movie world of the film, shows us that Ranse and Hallie leave *before*, and so do not attend, Tom's funeral. Something the conductor says implies there is a tight train connection, but that hardly seems persuasive. Tom will be buried, probably in a pauper's grave, attended only by Pompey, since his important friends have to rush off somewhere for another appointment.) In their conversation on the train, Ranse proposes to Hallie that they not resettle in Washington but come back to Shinbone for their final years. She answers as if very moved, and confesses that her "roots" are in Shinbone, indeed that her "heart is here." She also remarks as she looks out the window that what was once a wilderness is now a garden, and she asks a question that seems to take in all of modernity, and thereby becomes a deep and disturbing question to the audience, the answer to which is not obvious: "Aren't you proud?"

Somehow that at least does not seem to be important for Ranse, as if the technological and engineering and commercial accomplishments do not touch the real issue, don't of themselves prove anything about what really has been achieved. (This had been suggested in Hallie's conversation with Link. She marvels in that conversation at the schools, churches, and shops, and seems to be thinking of Ranse's accomplishments. But Link, in a way that seems deflating, says only that "the railroad done that" [as if to say, *not* Ranse], and he remarks, as though anticipating what Hallie will say later on the train, that "the desert is *the same*.") Ranse doesn't respond to Hallie as his demeanor (which suggests extreme vanity) would lead us to expect. He doesn't respond at all and turns to a much more human and complicated issue. He asks her who put the cactus roses on Tom's coffin.[31]

The fact that it was Hallie seems to upset him. Is he thinking that not only are Shinbone and the state and his career built on a lie, but his whole life is, that the belief that he had won Hallie away from Tom might be just as deceptive? What must have being going through his mind when she said that her heart is in the desert? Here, not in Washington and London and all those years with Ranse. (As far as we know, the marriage between Hallie and Ranse is childless; in this context it might be called "barren," and it would be understandable if Hallie were thinking about what a life with Tom on the ranch, perhaps with children, would have been. That might be a good part of the deep melancholy that surrounds them, and that surrounds the sterility and deadness of the new Shinbone.)

Their exchange also returns us to elements of the opening whose significance we can now better understand, the oddness of which we can now better appreciate. If we remember the opening, we must be struck even more by Ranse's question about who put the cactus roses on Tom's coffin. Who else could it have been, and why is he puzzled? Here was Hallie, carting around a huge, empty hatbox all the way from St. Louis, keeping it separate from the rest of their luggage and carrying it with her even on the initial buckboard ride with Link, and it appears never to have occurred to Ranse to ask her what that was for, and it never occurred to him to draw the simple inference that it must have been for the cactus rose. Not to mention that in some respects the desert did not need to be made into a garden; it already had its own roses.

And that suspicion is intensified as we and Ranse are reminded one final time that he owes everything he has achieved to a heroic legendary accomplishment that never happened. The conductor intones the closing lines, "Nothing is too good for the Man Who Shot Liberty Valance," and Stoddard blows out his match, as if something of value has been extinguished in this new world. There is no great puff of smoke, in contrast to

3.9

Tom's flashback. There is not much interpretive ambiguity here, as there was about what Tom's action and sacrifice meant. Ranse did not shoot Liberty Valance, and he has lived his life as if he had (fig. 3.9).

VII

To understand where we are left, we have to return to the male triangle again, and the woman who waits for it to be resolved: Ranse-Tom-Valance, that is, bourgeois civility and law on one end; anarchistic violence, near-animal brutality, and hedonism on the other; and the mediating figure of Tom, in both worlds. We come closer to understanding where the film leaves us by appreciating that it is at its core a tragedy, a mythically significant or representative tragedy, and that the main figure of this tragedy is Tom Doniphon. He does what needs to be done silently and selflessly, disappearing into history, not honored in any legend, not mythologized, not even remembered. Partly this is because what needed to be done (a murder) cannot be the stuff of legend, but we should be clear on how complicated and thought-out Tom's act was. He could have stepped out of the shadows and made Ranse's fight his own; challenged Valance there in the street and finished him off in a "fair fight." But he of course recalls Ransom's fury when he did intervene in the restaurant ("Nobody fights my battles") and appreciates that such an intervention here would be even more emasculating. The representative of legal order must have his own status, his own honor. Even so, it would be a perfectly appropriate way of doing what Hallie has asked (and again she clearly asks more like a mother than a lover); under these circumstances no one could blame him for trying to show up Stoddard. He would have saved his life and done exactly what Hallie has asked. But Tom opts for what he thinks Hallie wants, what will make her happy, what will make the world she apparently wants possible. That is, in the political logic of the film, he opts for everything Hallie wants, that the desert become a garden, that there be schools, culture, normal commerce (that small horse ranchers become marginal and that politicians run things). Modern civilized life and modern political life is in some sense shown to depend on such private gestures and sacrifices, forgotten by history but nevertheless the historical reality of this transition.

Tom of course also seems to know that this is not ultimately a matter of what he or Hallie or Ranse want, that the end of the old Shinbone and of Tom's cultural code—self-sufficiency, honor, chivalry, simple pride in a "good job of work"—is historically inevitable. So he not only submits, he sacrifices himself and his own happiness for it. But Ford wants us to see what this cost him.

This has something of the same meaning as the end of *High Noon*. The film would have been entirely different (although such an alternative is a plausible possibility) if in some scene Tom had said to Hallie something like: "Shinbone will never grow or prosper or be safe as long as Valance and the cattle barons keep this area a territory, not a state, and so hold onto power. Valance must be dealt with and I'll do it." As in *High Noon,* the *psychological* reality of political life turns out to be bonds not themselves political but private and romantic, only indirectly and secondarily political. They are crucial to political life, but our stake in a political fate is not only mediated and motivated by such affective bonds, it is wholly dependent on and fueled by them. Marshal Kane tries to avoid the role of hero and asks for collective action. But at the end what matters is his wife's loyalty.

Consider by contrast what the "legend" has brought us to. One should not be too hard on Ransom Stoddard, for he is an awfully brave man, and he certainly seems to believe what he says about words, books, rules, and law, and Ford clearly admires this commitment to law. (Although it does not seem unfair to note that Ranse believes in these things because they are his weapons; he knows he can win with them if his society becomes the new Shinbone we see at the film's beginning. Ranse went west to make his fortune as a lawyer, not to be a social reformer. "I don't want to kill him," he says about Valance. "I want to put him in jail." It is as if he is trying to threaten Valance with his own "guns.") It is, though, a stunning revelation when we see the great difference in his roles as senator and as a private man talking with his wife, when we see him hooking his thumbs in his vest and speechifying at every opportunity, and when we realize that it seems to be dawning on him that his wife not only once deeply loved Tom Doniphon but that she may love him still, throughout and after all these years. And Ranse's own confrontation with Valance is also not itself accompanied by any rhetoric of politics. His own pride, especially given his unacknowledged competition with Tom for Hallie, and his friendship with the badly beaten Peabody, seem to have as much to do with his bravery as anything else, however brave he truly is.

The problem is that he doesn't seem the kind of man who will admit this to himself, admit that political reality in a mass democracy is not reality (he buys his own legend at some level). Recall that in their conversation on the train Hallie had responded to his suggestion that they retire to Shinbone by saying, "Oh, Ranse, if you knew how many times I've dreamed of that . . ." They have lived together for all these years and Ranse never knew this? One suspects it is because he had never thought to ask. And again this private and romantic issue carries some political meaning. It goes to the root of Ranse's lack of self-knowledge, a certain blindness about the costs to be incurred by the kind of order he proposes for the town, by the kind of world he wanted for himself and Hallie. (None of this yet touches on the further complication: that the film ends with the creation of yet another self-deception—the idea that they will return to Shinbone and set up a small law practice and a little garden. The Shinbone they want to return to is as dead as Tom Doniphon in his coffin; as dead as the old West of independence and honor loved by Ford.)[32]

If evidence is needed about what this has cost Hallie (what Ranse has escaped only by a certain blindness) we can return to the opening conversation between Hallie and a considerably more dignified and serious Link than the narration shows.

Two things are of importance in their conversation on the buckboard. The first is what was noted in passing above. We have just heard (in the final scene) Hallie express the cliché that the old Shinbone that was a desert is now a garden. But we hear Link say just the opposite; he notes that while much has changed, "the desert is the same." There are some things modernization cannot touch or change. Second, it is obvious that Link alone appreciates what this homecoming must mean for Hallie. This is another way of saying that he (alone) knows what she gave up for the world she wanted (or thought she wanted); that she perhaps gave up the love of her life. He knows this; she clearly knows he knows, and he knows that she knows he knows. Hence the quiet tension in the scene. The two points are then nicely connected by the cactus rose symbol; on the one hand it is of the never really changing desert, and on the other a figure for Hallie's never changing even if sacrificed love.

We also need to take fully on board the fact that Ranse, for all his high-mindedness, is willing, without much visible struggling with his conscience, to build his life on a lie. In a simple word, this is dishonorable, and there is no question that Ford wants us to see that it is dishonorable, even if it is also partly excusable. What is not excusable on such a reading would be pretending that no price had been paid for security, peace, and prosperity. And Ranse does seem guilty of this forgetfulness, at least up until this point in the story.[33] But we get no clear indication of why he has chosen at this moment to tell the true story, especially since there appears to be some chance that he will be a vice-presidential candidate. When he parts from Hallie to talk with the journalists he tells Hallie only that he is going to "mend some political fences." (Perhaps he means that he wants to make peace with his own conscience.) But there is no sign on the face of the impassive, sad Hallie that she realizes what he is actually proposing to do. In fact, there is no sign that she knows at all that the Valance myth is a lie. At the conductor's last words on the train, she registers no reaction. It is Ranse who looks grieved and chastened. His demeanor when the editor tells him that he will not use the story is also unusual. He does not act at all surprised, almost as if he were expecting such a reaction. His tone is one of an assumed invulnerability and is consistent with the pomposity and falseness that infuses all his public comments.

Ford is not an innocent here. He seems to be acknowledging the "way of the world" and the fact of political necessity and compromise and fantasy in modern commercial republics, but he clearly thinks that there is a big difference between a reluctant concession to political reality, one always qualified by concerns about integrity and honesty, restrained by skepticism, and

3.10

3.11

going so far as to *lose* the distinction between legend and fact. As the newspaper editor crumples up and throws away the notes he has taken—the "true story"—we are clearly meant to think back on the drunk and also very brave Peabody, who was willing to pay the price for printing the truth about Liberty Valance.

We are meant to recall Valance stuffing his newspaper into his mouth. In effect, the contemporary editor is doing voluntarily what had to be *forced* on Peabody (figs. 3.10 and 3.11).

VIII

This would suggest that, just as in *Red River*, Bazin's useful notion of seeing Westerns as modern mythology has to be qualified a bit. The two films discussed here might better be called examples of mythological modernism, for the level of reflection, self-consciousness, self-thematization, and even irony is much higher than is usually attributed to Westerns or to myths. That is, *The Man Who Shot Liberty Valance* is not itself a mythological treatment of a founding. It is rather about mythological accounts of foundings (indeed about the distorting and self-serving effects of even normal narration), and it is quite a qualified, even skeptical cautionary account of such mythologizings, despite Ford's reputation for believing the idealizations he puts in the mouths of his characters. (With some judiciously placed quotation marks, "The man who *shot* 'Liberty Valance'" would have to be John Ford himself.) The oddly unattractive picture of modern Shinbone, with the rough edges smoothed out but stale, cold, too quiet; what the fact of Tom's death has forced Ranse and Hallie to confront; and what we learn of the burden Hallie has lived with all suggest such a reflective and distancing characterization.

Let us for a moment indulge the contentious and complicated notion that a film itself can, by virtue of the unitary vision
of its author, be said to have a point of view on the events nar-
rated, that we can be said in some sense to be guided toward
a certain assessment of what we have seen and away from others.
The film we are considering suggests that one of the psychological requirements necessary for a shared political identification is a heroizing narrative about a common origin and the
bravery and sacrifices of the original founders. But then all the
qualifications are also suggested. This glorifying legend is also
quite likely a fantasy, and there will come a time when the less
than glorious truth must out, or when it at least powerfully
threatens to be revealed. There is a high cost to pay for continuing the lie under these circumstances. It is dishonorable and
unworthy of a great civilization to continue to indulge such fantasies. It blinds us to the less legendary but more everyday and
real accomplishments and sacrifices of those forgotten by such
accounts and especially to those victimized by such a founding
(something Ford would try hard, probably too hard, to remind
his viewers of in films like *Cheyenne Autumn*). And most of all
such self-inflating stories blind us to what *we* have lost, what
was given up, in a transition to a particular form of civilized
authority, a commercial republic.

At the end of the film, no one wants his or her positions of
power, wealth, and influence threatened, and the plausible assumption is that political life in its infancy is fragile and easily

lost without such stories of good and evil. ("This is the West . . ."
is the editor's preface for his legend/fact conflation.) So they col-
lude in a continuation of the fantasy. We are not left with the
suggestion that it would be an easy thing to try to remember
Tom Doniphon in our historical narrative, and not just Ranse
Stoddard, or that our political world can simply dispense with
legends and instead institutionalize more prosaic and more morally complicated narratives, but the presence of the film itself,
with its unmistakable air at the end of "ideology critique" (to use
a term I doubt has been used before in discussions of Ford) at
least suggests that the cost of continuing such blindness is too
high. Hallie is the figure for that price. It is not, in other words,
the relative thinness of political culture in modern America that
is so much the problem. There might indeed be a problem holding together a society more inclined toward Tom's mode of being
in the world than Ranse's, and without our legends a pretty prosaic world would come to look even more prosaic, raising psychological questions about its sustainability as a political
enterprise. But the passion for something more—more glorious,
larger than life, mythic, a common destiny, a world historical
mission—is, I would suggest, treated here as the greater danger.

IX

One sometimes hears it said that the great thing about Westerns
is their moral clarity: black hats and white hats, bad guys and

good guys, and morally uplifting tales of the victory of good guys over bad guys, a victory achieved by dint of the virtues of the hero and the vices of the villain. This might have been true of TV shows like *Gunsmoke* and 90 percent of "B" Westerns, but it certainly is not true of the work of directors like Ford, Hawks, Mann, Boetticher, Daves, Zinnemann, Wyler, King, Fuller, Walsh, Vidor, Peckinpah, or Ray. In fact, just the opposite is often true. Their Westerns are more like noirs than children's adventure stories or action pictures.[34] What *is* true is that their presentations of conflict, hesitations, ambiguity, and crises largely concern characters trying to resolve issues of right, justice, responsibility, honor, and the claims of the public world versus the private, and that these situations are presented in both historical and psychological terms that greatly complicate any neat moral dividing line between characters, any straightforward assessments of events. The historical dimension means that many of the better films are exploring something like the psychological adequacy of various political aspects of new industrialized mass societies and the attendant politics of these societies, are exploring the psychological and ethical meaning of "the end of the frontier." By psychological adequacy, I simply mean that the films are treating the question of whether it is good or ultimately even possible for the human soul to live this way, not that way, in the world that Stoddard brings to Shinbone, and not the world left behind of Tom Dunson and Tom Doniphon, all even if ultimately no one has any choice in the matter. The fact that the rule

of law and equal protection under the law is more universally
justifiable can itself be a powerful element in the establishment
of that law. There is such a thing as the politics of truth.[35] But the
way in which such claims of reason become part of a living and
reproducible political culture are various and complex, and we
have not done much of the hard or interesting work in political
thought if we note merely that Ranse's position is the true one
and Liberty's not. The interesting work begins when we note that
if Ranse were "armed" only with "the truth" Liberty would have
made short work of him.

One can think of that question of psychological adequacy
this way. It is a kind of cliché that in revolutionary situations,
in wars foreign and civil, and in the chaos of foundings and
great historical transitions, political passions can be inspired
more easily and political issues can come to be of more burning
concern than in peaceful, ordinary situations. If politics is possible, it requires some sort of commitment, some sort of dedication to one another, to strangers, just as fellow citizens, and it is
easier to imagine all that being a live issue when a community is
under threat, tearing itself apart, terrorized by the lawless at
home. Westerns like *Liberty Valance* help us see the role of such
crises and the attendant psychological complications. But the
best of them, like *Liberty Valance*, also raise of the question of
post-crisis political psychology too, especially by vivid contrast,
especially for the particular case of bourgeois commercial republics. Even though there is a long tradition of worry about

violent passions (and "the mob") playing a role in politics, it is a dangerously naïve fantasy to believe that, other than in these "states of exception," everyday political allegiance is created and reinforced by deliberative procedures guided by a common appeal to reason. Our newspaper editor is not wrong to worry about Shinbone, so clean and empty and quiet, without its legends.[36] What kind of dedication and commitment could *that* way of life inspire on its own? But it surely cannot be irrelevant to Ford's vision that whatever the useful psychological function of the legend, it is a *lie* (in this film we are close to the suggestion that "the law" itself is a lie), and it is ever more difficult over time to live with a lie.

I am not sure where, if anywhere, this leaves us. But there is a psychological state of great importance to politics not yet discussed, the sheer force of which threatens to make all other aspects of human political psychology irrelevant. It is hatred, and there is a very complicated Western about hate, John Ford's *The Searchers*.

4 POLITICS AND SELF-KNOWLEDGE IN *THE SEARCHERS*

I

I HAVE been arguing that great Hollywood Westerns explore in a large mythic framework (where mythic self-consciousness is an attempt at a form of collective self-knowledge) representations and enactments of the political psychology characteristic of a distinctly American imaginary, and that this imaginary both concerns and is itself central to the nature of the political in the American experience. This has meant that the films, in their own filmic and self-conscious way, direct our attention to characteristic psychological attitudes, aspirations, and anxieties constitutive of a historical political actuality; they focus attention on the self-representations of political agents themselves. There is often special attention given to situations "internal" to the movie world where such attempts at self-knowledge fail in distinctive ways, where some representation of commitments or ideals or just claims about one's own attitudes do not match up with what is in fact done or pursued, or where the best explanation of what does occur must invoke some self-deceit or blindness in characters' avowals of such ideals or claims. I have suggested, that is, that the films themselves are not examples of the mythologizing of the West and the fate of such attempted mythologizing; the great ones are almost always about this.

So in Hawks's *Red River* we get a myth about how a patriarchal and charismatic form of rule is overthrown and replaced by a fraternal, humanistic, and egalitarian form of rule, one that is clearly supposed to be close to our own avowed commitments. But the movie occurs right after the Civil War, a fratricidal war of such great savagery that we have reason to be skeptical about claims of fraternal harmony, and the character who embodies this self-representation seems actually to be a more efficient form of the tyrant he replaced. In *The Man Who Shot Liberty Valance* there is an attempt to come to terms with a kind of point now associated with Carl Schmitt—that the establishment of any legal order, of whatever doctrine, even liberal-democratic and humanist, must be illegal, violent, unjust, and brutal, and a society must find a way to represent that fact to itself as a national memory. It usually does this, as in this picture, by lying, by a distorting mythologizing, and there is even some suggestion that the lie involves the basic promise that there is such a thing as the political. (If one accepts that *Tom* killed Liberty Valance, the episode is only another cycle of private passion and revenge, and politics looks like nothing but the temporary victory of one group over another. That *Ranse* killed Liberty Valance can mean that his ideals—the rule of law and democratic politics—triumphed. But Ranse did not kill Liberty Valance. This may be a lie we have to live with, but there is a subtle suggestion in the film that this is a very high price to pay. The figure for that price in all sorts of complicated ways is Hallie.)

And in *The Searchers* there is a direct confrontation with the fact that the origin of the territorial United States rests on a virulent racism and genocidal war against aboriginal peoples, a war that would not have been possible and perhaps would not have been won without the racist hatred of characters like the John Wayne character. The official avowal *now* is that we regret this and have overcome such attitudes. But the film manages to raise a number of questions concerning the relation between such avowals about having transcended the past and about what is done or not done in the present. But to show this I need to turn to the film. I will begin with another generalization about Westerns very much on view in *The Searchers* and quite important for the classic Westerns made by John Ford.

II

There is very little romanticism in many of the great Hollywood Westerns, including Ford's. The core narrative in many films involves three basic elements, in varying degrees underlying or explicit in the plots. One concerns the conquest by force of arms of an aboriginal people, and these people are not represented as innocent or naturally good or gentle. They are understandably resisting with ferocious violence the seizure of their land and a campaign of extermination, and they are often portrayed as a warrior people by nature, as if to make the point that the state of nature is the state of war.[1] Sometimes their willingness to risk life and their devotion to honor is contrasted with the often craven mentality of the invading whites, to the obvious detriment of those settlers. The cowboys who are portrayed as heroic are most often associated with the Indian virtues of honor, loyalty, and courage.[2] The doomed fate of both the Indians and the heroic cowboys is often treated mythically as the doomed fate of these very traits and virtues in the modern world, a world now complex enough to require a level of cooperation, compromise, prudence, bet-hedging, and repression that is inimical to such states of the soul.

A second narrative concerns the conquest by labor, persistence, violence, and technology of an extraordinarily hostile, inhospitable natural world, as much an enemy of human civilization as a demonic, angry god. (Ford's Monument Valley landscapes make this point with immediate, visually compelling power.) One could put the point about the violent conquest of nature this way: we speak of the "American founding," but America has been founded several times. Narratives of the original colonization and rebellion were often accompanied by images of Eden and innocence destroyed or lost, promised or redeemed; and they were all bloody. The Civil War required another new, and a new type of, violent founding, an attempt at reconciliation that many Westerns often imply was a failure. And then there is the conquest of the West and the Indian wars, the founding of the continental United States and the westward expansion. Here the shift from images of forest and meadow to rock and sand reframes the mythic self-image of America and suggests the need for a new and much more complicated hero, but the "conquest of hostile nature" theme remains constant.

And a third narrative concerns what could be called the conquest of inner nature, the need to establish a stable political order and thereby some strategy for the suppression of those passions both hostile to and yet often central in politics that are released in the lawless situation of the West, and the suppression (and yet use) of those individuals given to those passions. These are all obviously also linked because, given the stereotypical way Indians are presented, all three "enemies" are at bottom the same enemy: nature. The outlaw passion that humans are naturally heir to is treated with remarkable, even crude, frankness in *The Searchers*. It is explosive and still all too familiar: racism and racial hatred. The questions raised by the film concern the origin and meaning of racial and ethnic hatred, the effect of such hatred on the possibility of communal life, the role played by racial identification in forging the social bond necessary for political life, and, especially, the prospects of overcoming such passions, both racial passions and the passions inflamed by any war, especially a fratricidal war like the American Civil War. (The framework of *The Searchers* thus poses a question about politics and political psychology that would have again been familiar to Carl Schmitt: the role of the enemy and the resources of modern bourgeois societies for dealing with the enemy. It also treats an issue Schmitt was not terribly concerned about but should have been: the destabilizing and politically uncontrollable aspects of a world dominated by friend-enemy distinctions.)

And so, as noted, the framework within which these questions are asked is not a romantic one. Nature in all the senses mentioned is hostile, the greatest enemy, dangerous and treacherous, and any successful political redemption from human passions that we are subject to by nature will have to be the result of a long and unpredictable struggle. Or at least that is the self-understanding of the characters and the meaning of the visual images given us by Ford.

III

The Searchers is one of the greatest and most ambitious films ever made, and so of course it is impossible to summarize it simply. Although a half a dozen things are going on in each scene, I will focus on one issue of relevance to the theme of politics and political psychology. The main character, played (in his greatest role) by John Wayne, is Ethan Edwards, a Civil War veteran (a displaced and wandering southerner, a "Texican") returning in the film's majestic opening scene to his brother Aaron's small, somewhat pathetic cattle ranch in south Texas. We learn—elliptically and indirectly—that Ethan had been very probably fighting as a mercenary for the Emperor Maximilian in Mexico in the three years after the Civil War, and that he may be wanted by American authorities for something or other.[3] He has a great deal of money on him, the origin of which is never explained. The main conflict in the movie, its main mystery, is very much a kind of epistemological problem of great relevance to any political reflection, and it is immediately and dramatically raised for those who greet the mysterious and opaque Ethan at the beginning. It is: *understanding Ethan,* something that turns out to be extremely difficult if not impossible.[4] The very first word of the movie sums up its question: "Ethan?" And Ethan, as the Reverend Clayton says, "fits a lot of descriptions."[5] Since Ethan is both a powerfully disruptive force and an agent of change and even perhaps reconciliation, this question of how to understand him, even what it would be to understand him or anyone, becomes more than a question about an individual's psychology.

Ethan is on a quest that seems to border on something insane (that is, until we realize that he actually embodies, even represents, a shared, hidden mindedness in his community). And he brings that quest to an end in a way that makes us doubt whether we have ever understood him, whether he has ever even understood himself, whether the self-knowledge called for in political life, something like a community's self-knowledge, is ever possible. Given the larger-than-life and mythic dimensions of the narrative, the problem of how to understand Ethan is also linked to the question of the viewers' understanding of our own history, suffused as so much of it is with racial hatred and the promise of its overcoming.

Ford goes very far with Ethan—so far that it is hard to imagine how he thought he could get away with it. A central character who spews racist invective at every opportunity, who mutilates the bodies of the dead, shooting out the eyes of a dead Indian and scalping an adversary, even though he did not "earn" that warrior right by killing him himself, who slaughters buffalo in an insane rage just to deprive Indians of food, and who is out to murder a child? He is probably a criminal, even though, paradoxically, he seems uninterested in money. How could such a story ever be "pitched" to a studio head? (Not to mention that Ethan interrupts funerals, scoffs at religion, uses racial epithets like "blanket-head," shoots both whites and Indians in the back, and runs over women and children when on horseback.) It is clearly a great experiment, one that baffled and angered the early critics. But Ford is also at his most ambitious here, setting out a Conradean framework as sweeping as *Heart of Darkness*, in which an outward quest or search figures the search within, the place of Ethan's heart of darkness. True to all great works of art, nothing is resolved, and the ending scene is as complex as the fiction that the narrator invents and reports to the beloved in Conrad's novella.

IV

The film opens in a way that is mysterious, obviously ambitious, and strangely tense, fraught with poorly concealed anxiety. Many things have been written about the opening, especially about how quickly it establishes Ethan as "outsider," that our orienting shot is from inside hearth and home, a space with no place for a man like Ethan, even though he will be desperately needed by the "insiders." The attempt at a kind of royal or operatic grandeur in the staging is unmistakable; the characters almost ritualistically slowly move to what seem assigned spots for the entrance of the monarch, all to the point of Martha awkwardly withdrawing backward into the house, as if before a king to whom subjects must never show their back sides. And there is the remarkable tension already present in a much too formal, too staged kiss on the forehead, our first signal that this is not a typical cheery homecoming (figs. 4.1–4.3; plates 1–3).

We will quickly learn two things about the mysterious man, still draped in the uniform of the defeated South. He is consumed by racial hatred of Indians, and he covets his brother's wife.[6] Perhaps there is a third thing that links these two,

4.1

4.2

4.3

although this is never made explicit by dialogue or event: he seems consumed by guilt and self-hatred about this lust, which may have something to do with racism. (Making this connection between sexual self-doubt and self-hatred and the projection of just what he hates about what he wants to do onto "the Other," and so with racism, was also a remarkable suggestion for a commercial film in 1956.)

The complications in Ethan's racial hatred—that he also identifies with what he hates—will soon be established visually by a simple, very visible prop: the Indian rifle scabbard that Ethan always carries, and more tellingly by his intimate knowledge and apparent acceptance of Comanche religion. Here in the opening scene some of that complication (what some now call "hybridity" between occupier and occupied) is presaged by the marks of contact between or interpenetration between Indian and white culture signaled by those prominent blankets in the opening and soon by the mixed-race status of the boy who will become his searching companion, Martin Pawley.[7]

There is a famous scene that establishes that there is an illicit sexual desire that is not incidental to Ethan's wild rages, but it is so subtle that it was missed by many early critics.[8] Ward Bond's character, who is both a captain in the Texas Rangers and the local pastor, enters the cabin. (This small bit of political theology is another bold characterization. It suggests at once both that the law's legitimacy might not be sufficient to command alle-

4.4

giance without the "ideological" support of the good book, and that in this violent world religious authority must have some teeth, be backed by bullets, if it is to exercise any actual authority.)[9] Some cattle have been rustled and a posse is being formed to hunt the thieves. This is another much commented-on scene, as it establishes indirectly that the Ethan-Martha attraction is hidden, even if in plain sight. (They are somewhat reckless with their looks.) It is also a signal that everything we are about to see might be treated as the captain/clergyman treats what he sees, in knowing ignorance, or we could choose to "look" at what no one inside the film wants to look at (fig. 4.4; plate 4).

We quickly discover that the cattle rustling was a feint by the Indians to draw the ranchers and Rangers away so they could attack the ranch of Martha and Aaron. They do attack, kill Aaron and his son, abduct Lucy and Debbie, and rape and

4.5

kill Martha. (We should note, by the way, that it is clear in the film that Ethan could have stayed instead of taking Aaron's place with the posse. Mose Harper had already sounded the warning that these were Comanches on a raid, not ordinary cattle rustlers. Ethan may be acting out his bitterness over having lost Martha to Aaron; as if saying, "You, Martha, chose him as your protector, so let him protect you." The family does mention, in a plaintive, pathetic way, that they wish Ethan were there, and not Aaron. This may feed into the obvious self-hatred and great guilt visible in Ethan's quest. But for his pride and resentment, he might have saved them.)

Ethan, Mose, and Martin discover the burned-out ranch and find Martha's body. Ford uses for the second time the "inside looking out from the dark" shot that had opened the film, this time from inside the small hut where Martha lies (fig. 4.5; plate 5).

The discovery of Martha's raped body is certainly shocking and horrific enough all by itself to generate Ethan's desire for revenge, but the hints we have been given about him and Martha suggest that some of this rage is tied to his own guilt and self-hatred. His love for Martha was after all deeply illicit; not only was she married, she was married to his brother, and yet he desired her still (and the love seems to have been reciprocated). One way or another everything in the film will turn on this fact, its meaning and the way its implications are lived out. It is biblical in its force here; something like the Ur-drama of civilized repression, worked out around the marriage promise and the question of whether such a promise and so the establishment of perhaps *the* civilized norm, all in the face of one of the most powerful passions, is possible, and, if so, how. Ethan accepts the sanctity of the institution (it seems clear that neither he nor Martha ever acted on their passion), but the irrational explosions that such acceptance spawns constantly unsettle everything.[10] He is a kind of walking manifestation of the costs incurred by the repression necessary for civilized life, and his eruptions of hatred, revenge, racism, and blind fury are tied to these inner dynamics as much as they are to the external threats and projects of the "official" or conscious civilized world. (When Ethan later interrupts the comically inappropriate marriage of Laurie and Charlie, we are perhaps meant to think of it as recalling Martha's mistaken choice in opting for Aaron.)[11]

4.6

The deputized group starts off after the Indians, and they and we are startled by Ethan's ferocity when they discover an Indian body that his comrades have hastily buried. When Brad, the captured Lucy's intended, hurls a rock at the dead Indian in fury and frustration, Ethan calmly, and with a sarcastic edge to his voice, says, "Why don't you finish the job?" He draws his pistol and shoots the corpse in the eyes and explains that for the Comanche this means that the brave will not be able to enter the spirit land. ("Ain't got no eyes, he can't enter the spirit land, must wander forever between the winds.")

The eerie "signing" by Mose Harper of what Ethan is saying about wandering suggests some commonality between Ethan's and Mose's near-madness, even as it also establishes the seriousness with which he takes Indian beliefs (fig. 4.6; plate 6). It also manifests again the hatred/self-hatred theme, since the description of someone who must wander endlessly between the winds fits Ethan more than anyone.[12] It is telling that this wandering and homelessness is linked to blindness ("ain't got no eyes, he can't enter the spirit land"), an emergence of the self-knowledge theme again. (Ethan clearly thinks he hates Indians because they killed some white people he knew. But he hates all Indians, and, like all of Ethan's attitudes, this is held in a kind of silence, without reflection or justification. It is a striking thing about the film that Ethan never makes a racist speech, never explains, even to himself, why his attitude seems so much like Kurtz's in *Heart of Darkness* ("kill them all"). He generalizes about Indians, but there is no sloganeering or racist theorizing. It is a brilliant move by Ford and the screenwriter, Frank Nugent: we are called on to provide what Ethan cannot or will not. And it is consistent with so many unknowns intimated visually, demanding some pursuit of purely visual intelligibility: Why is Ethan dressed as he is? What has he been doing? What did he and Martha do or not do, before or after her marriage? What was Ethan's relation to Martin's parents? What happened when Ethan found Lucy? What about the long close-ups of Ethan and Scar? And what is the meaning of Ethan's famous gesture at the end, raising Debbie once again above his head?

The search begins for Lucy (who is soon discovered raped and killed) and the youngest, Debbie. There is a small piece of stage business that Wayne performs after the discovery of Lucy,

4.7

a very brief scene, but it indicates the visual suggestiveness of virtually everything in the film. When Ethan returns from the canyon where he has discovered Lucy's body and buried her, he takes out his knife and begins furiously digging in the earth (fig. 4.7; plate 7).

Why have Ethan dig with his knife so violently in the earth after discovering a rape? Of course Ethan has not been fantasizing about raping Lucy or Martha, but I think there are plenty of indications that he regards himself, as the lover of his brother's wife, as not much better than such a rapist. He could be remembering "burying her with his own hands," as he admits later, but if so, the part of the burial he remembers is instructive. His acting out this violent penetration of the earth seems to call to mind such wholly unreasonable and extreme guilt.

It is hard to establish the exact number of years covered by the search; most commentators count five, though some count seven, from the time Debbie is nine until she is sixteen. The great shock of the movie begins when we realize that Ethan is trying to find Debbie (the very young daughter of the woman he obviously loved dearly) not to rescue her but to kill her. He seems to believe that any white girl raised to be an Indian squaw would be better off dead, although, as noted, this is never articulated as such; it is the brutality of this intention and the ferocity and near insanity with which it is pursued that stuns the viewer and prompts the attempt to understand who this man is. Martin (played by Jeffrey Hunter) stays with him not merely to help him find her but to be there when they do, so he can stop this.

It is important to note that this is not all about Ethan's peculiar, individual neurosis. A "national character" is one defined against others, against real or imagined enemies, and this sort of hatred is not peculiar to Ethan. Vera Miles plays an interesting role in the movie as Laurie, the longtime friend of Martin. They were obviously assumed always to be meant for each other, and there is one stunning scene that establishes the generality of the problem of Ethan, and which suggests that Ethan is not the crazy outsider or the dark and repressed side of this white American society. He is its representative. In the scene Laurie is dressed in virginal white. This is her wedding day (she has given up waiting for Martin), and we are once again faced with a core civilizational promise: that sexual desire be regulated, confined to marriage, and we face again the fragility and uncertainty of

4.8

such promises to control the passions. Clad in such virginal white, Laurie also seems to hold the most innocent, unreflectively held and common views from her world. In many ways this revelation is even more shocking to the viewer than the knowledge that Ethan is out to kill Debbie.[13]

When Martin insists that he must leave again to continue the search, Laurie responds with, "Fetch what home? The leavings of Comanche bucks, sold time and again to the highest bidder, with savage brats of her own? Do you know what Ethan will do if he has a chance? He'll put a bullet in her brain! I tell you Martha would want it that way" (fig. 4.8; plate 8).

We will see later that Laurie's attitude is not atypical. When the Reverend Clayton's posse is poised for the final attack, no one is at all concerned that, as Martin immediately points out, Debbie will be killed if they simply attack with full force. It takes him a while to persuade them to let him try to save her first.[14]

V

With this much of the film in view, I want now to start to ad-dress the issue of understanding Ethan, and the roles of psycho-logical knowledge and self-knowledge in political life. Once the viewer is over the shock of learning that Ethan is planning on murdering a perfectly innocent and already long-suffering sixteen-year-old girl, we come to think we know something about him, although much remains shrouded in mystery. We at least think we know something of the ferocity and near insanity of his sentiments, and the content or object of his passions. The scene in which Ethan shoots out the eyes of the dead Comanche already establishes how much Ethan knows about the Coman-ches, and why. (We are close to a point noted by many film crit-ics: the chief Indian character, Scar [the one who steals Debbie] sometimes seems another part of Ethan's character, his alter ego, that part of him we need to understand to understand him. All as if Ethan has projected an emanation [in the Blakean sense] of himself, everything illicit that he nevertheless devoutly wants, such that, by killing Scar, Ethan will prove that those desires were never part of him. They are in fact mirror or twinned char-acters in many ways. They are both on ferocious revenge quests;

4.9

Ethan wants to do to Scar what he imagines Scar did to him, steal and kill his "woman"; and they both seem hybrid characters, as in their conversation about Comanche and English.)

Ethan and Martin at one point come upon a group of soldiers who have found some captive white girls, and that occasions one of the most important scenes in the movie, a scene that is about the intimate relation between the face and the human soul that is behind the great emotional power of close-ups. Ford, well known for his classic stationary camera, also wants very much to heighten our attention to the *question* posed by this look, and so he zooms in; it is a rare moment of both motion and psychological intensity, as if the zoom in is a way of asking: What does this look mean (fig. 4.9; plate 9)?

The question of understanding Ethan is deeply interwoven with the question of how to interpret this singular, eerie look. It is not so much anger or hatred, even though there are profound flashes of that. Is there sadness at what he thinks he has to do? Self-hatred at not being able to feel the pity he knows he should? Wayne is the master of cold, reptilian looks in this film, but this is the extreme, and almost completely ambiguous. It clearly has something to do with the fragility of what makes up the content of a civilizational identity, the basis of a national or individual character. Ethan seems to look full in the face the mutability and instability of the "grip" of such civilizational values. One might even say that it is an archetypal modern anxiety. "All that is solid melts into air," Marx's famous characterization of modern experience, is evoked here by "She ain't white." (One of the most disturbing aspects for audiences of "captive literature" from the seventeenth century on was the not infrequent phenomenon of captive women who, when "rescued," chose to remain with the "savages." This obviously unsettles the notion of civilized order and its putative superiority, and part of this issue seems visible in "the look.")

The film's focus on kinship and adoption clearly resonates with the American civil rights issues of 1956. Ethan's position is quite complicated and unstable. He clearly believes, as a staunch defender of the Confederacy, that convention cannot alter the facts of nature, that it is not good by nature that races mix, that Martin's having been adopted and raised as white cannot change the fact that he is basically, for Ethan, colored, of Indian blood. Yet he also seems to believe that Debbie, while biologically white, could become so corrupted by Indian mores that she must be killed rather than saved. (As in this scene: "She ain't white.") In the later will and testament scene, Ethan also clearly believes that he can simply end his kinship relation with Debbie, as if it is a matter of some convention.[15] And, contrastingly, we see that by Indian law, Debbie is a wife among equals; she even seems a kind of princess. Contrast this with what both Martin and Ethan seem to regard as the utter and comic inconceivability of Martin's "marriage" to the Indian Look (whom Martin has mistakenly married in a trading agreement), who is treated as a figure of derision until they both must face what their attitude entails.[16]

This complex situation has a number of implications relevant to the meaning of the final Ethan-lifting-Debbie scene. It seems the reemergence of a kind of humanity in Ethan, but it could also represent the realization by him, as he looks into her eyes, that she is despite all (and for him, thankfully) *still white.* "Let's go home" could just emphasize this racial solidarity. Such a reading would also explain the absence of any full or satisfying reconciliation scene with Martin.[17]

We need a couple of final plot elements in order to return to the question of Ethan. Word reaches the searchers that Debbie is being held in an Indian encampment, and the army has joined the Texas Rangers and Ethan and Martin in preparation for a raid on this camp. This scene turns out to be one more and in effect the final piece of evidence in the puzzle of understanding

Ethan. We think we understand how his significant actions flow from a common source: his racism and self-hatred, his belonging more with Indians than whites, and his great discomfort with this, his guilt at his desire for his brother's wife, and so forth. Accordingly, we are not surprised when he is willing to attack the camp straight on, even though he and the others know this will result in Debbie's death. In fact, he says, "That's what I'm counting on." (Only shortly before this he had actually tried to shoot Debbie after they left the meeting with Scar. That is, even with Martin between them, Ethan fires. An Indian arrow hits him at the same time, but that is all that saves Debbie and Martin.) But now Martin persuades them all to allow him what seems a suicidal chance to rescue her before the attack. He does save her and shoots Scar in the process. That shot starts the general raid. During the course of the raid, Ethan finds Scar's tent, enters, draws his knife, and scalps Scar. He emerges from the tent with Scar's bloody scalp in his left hand, and yet again, Ford in effect pauses to concentrate on another extremely complicated, quite puzzling look on Ethan's face (fig. 4.10). We will return to this look in a moment.

So we think we are prepared for the final scene with Debbie and, in conventional movie logic, of course, we cannot believe that Ethan will kill Debbie, but I would wager that most of us expect Martin to stop him somehow (and certainly expect Ethan to kill Scar), and not for whatever internal transformation allows

4.10

Ethan to do what he does here. Ford shows us, for the third time, an inside-out shot, this time from inside a cave as Ethan rides down the fleeing Debbie. But we hear him call her name and know immediately that something has changed. It is not the tone of voice of an enraged man. And in the most famous scene in the film, he bends down and lifts her up in the air, exactly as he had lifted the young Debbie years earlier. But now he cradles her in his arms, and says simply, "Let's go home, Debbie." She hesitates but then nestles her head into his shoulder and they depart (figs. 4.11–4.13; plates 11–13).

VI

So we come again to the two mysteries posed by the movie: Why does Ethan seek to kill Debbie? And why *doesn't* Ethan kill Debbie?

4.11

4.12

4.13

There are some obvious possible answers for his unexpected return to recognizable humanity:

1. This could be a spontaneous, impulsive act, "out of character" but understandable in the way impulsive gestures sometimes are. That is, given what Ethan sincerely believes, this must count as a momentary act of "weakness"; ironically so, given that it is also morally praiseworthy, this inability of his to hold true to his racist principles. (In this respect it is like Huck Finn's guilt at not turning in Jim, even though he sincerely believes Jim is stolen property and that he is morally obligated to return him.)[18] Remarkably, in the shooting script for the movie the last scene involved the camera sighting down Ethan's gun barrel as he prepares to shoot Debbie, and he says, "You sure favor your mother."[19] And then he picks her up. Ford eliminated this all too easy explanation.

   But this appeal to impulsive charity does not seem likely. For one thing it just pushes the question back psychologically. Why, when he had drawn his gun and been prepared to shoot Debbie a bit before, stopped only by Martin and then an Indian arrow, and why, right after the most brutal enactment of racial hatred, his scalping Scar, would he feel this "weakness"? We have seen no evidence of such a side to Ethan's character, and it is far too easy an explanation. Acting on impulse, if it is still to be counted as acting, is motivated and intentional.

2. We might say that Ethan's basic character, his orientation, changes. Perhaps the long experience with Martin (whom he had originally considered a "half breed") and the gradual fading of his anger, self-hatred, and guilt, have now produced a more humane character.

   This is also not likely. The scalping scene certainly does not reveal a changed, kinder, gentler Ethan, and as we shall see, his eventual (understandable and justified) rejection by the social and familial world makes very difficult any transformation or redemption explanation. No one in the film believes he has changed into "Uncle Ethan," and we are clearly meant to agree. In the film's final scene it is somewhat shocking that the characters file by Ethan as if he were invisible. No one hugs him or thanks him, and certainly no one invites the "new" Ethan inside. (The shooting script had a reconciliation scene. Again, Ford eliminated it in favor of their ignoring him.[20])

3. There are two striking close-ups in the film: of Ethan in the Army hut with the white girls, and of Ethan's strange expression after scalping Scar (see figs. 4.9 and 4.10). We might read the latter as some sort of release. There is a look of puzzlement on Ethan's face, not a triumphalist gloating or even simple grim satisfaction. Does he believe that some score has now been settled? Does this bloody, brutal act strike his conscience, move him to back away from his violent intention? Is he confused that after achieving what he had wanted all these years, he does not feel satisfied, that he feels only empty and is puzzled at his lack of satisfaction?

   Ford leaves all this wonderfully and richly ambiguous. But I would suggest that the primary expression here is *puzzlement*, some indication that Ethan does not know his own mind, and suddenly realizes he does not know his own mind. And that brings us to a fourth alternative.

4. Perhaps we should start from the acknowledgment that the viewer by this point must have formed a view about Ethan, about his character, who he is, perhaps even about what he represents nationally or mythically, and has come to view him as simply a murderous, vile psychopath. Then our question changes. Of what significance is it that we were, if not wrong, then at least hasty? He does not "put a bullet in her brain," as the virginal Laurie had so enthusiastically suggested. Perhaps, having made the inference toward a generalization about "Ethan," we are learning that an inference *from* this generalization is radically uncertain and fraught with its own problems. (That is the most interesting question: Of what significance is it that Ethan's own expectations *about himself* turn out to be wrong?)

I mean something like the following. Ethan had clearly "formed the intention to kill Debbie." But we have seen that it is impossible to separate what that means for him—perhaps one can even say the full content of the intention—from (i) his illicit desire for his brother's wife and so his viewing himself as "like Scar," as "wanting to do what Scar did," to break apart his brother's family and steal Aaron's wife and children[21]; (ii) Ethan's natural sympathy for the martial, wandering, and heroic culture of Indians, even as he realizes (thinks he realizes) how unacceptable and "barbaric" this is; (iii) his projection of his own self-hatred onto Indians and so his desire to kill them all if he could, as proof to himself that these desires are not truly his; and thus (iv) his profound anxiety about miscegenation as apparently the worst human sin, as if such an extreme dedication to white racial purity could prove his civilized standing among whites despite his violent temptations. So while the intention seems simple enough, it is actually embedded in an extremely dense and relatively unstable complex of supporting attitudes and beliefs and remains largely provisional until Ethan must act. He will also be "proving something" by killing Debbie, "cleansing something" by killing Debbie, "expiating some guilt" by killing Debbie, "saving" Debbie from a fate worse than death, and so forth. None of these are properly "unconscious"; they are just indications at this point that he does not *merely* want *"to kill Debbie because she has been polluted or spoiled."*

We need a somewhat broader if very sketchy framework to appreciate this difficulty. Actions are purposive deeds, and we understand an action by understanding the intention avowed or manifested by an agent. Or at least we start there. We must also be able to understand something of the reasons that led an agent to the formation of such an intention. If we ask someone why he is methodically killing his relatives and he says, "I am killing them so that I might eat them and prevent the appearance of the angels," we would have literally understood his intention but not in a way that would render his action intelligible. So our attempt at understanding is always rationalizing, holistic, and psychological in this sense. The great problems occur when intentions do not match deeds, and when the question of what exactly was done becomes complicated and contested. That is our problem here.

I would suggest that Ethan has not acted impulsively nor revealed that he is weak-willed with respect to deeply held beliefs, nor that he has been transformed by the quest, nor that the scalping of Scar has shamed or humanized him. What we and he discover is that he did not know his own mind, that he avowed principles that were partly confabulations and fantasy. We (and he) find out the depth and extent of his actual commitments only when he finally must act. Moreover, we also learn how extraordinarily difficult it is to provide the proper act-description of just what it was that was done, to describe properly the quest in the first place and its unexpected ending, to measure how many psychological or social factors are involved in trying to say what Ethan did, and what he revealed, by saving rather than killing Debbie.

Now many philosophers will say that even though this—the multiple describability of actions—is true, the event qualifies as an action just in case it is intentional under some description *for the agent*, that what is relevant to understanding and explanation is the description the agent applied and so the intention formulated in its light. But this is still much too narrow. For one thing, with respect to understanding, such a proposal lands us back with "I am killing them so that I might eat them and prevent the appearance of the angels." It is hard to call understanding *that* understanding much of anything, and so it is hard to understand why the cold-blooded murder of a cherished innocent white child is required by some racist code. For another, agents themselves are often aware of the multiplicity of possible descriptions and have no clear sense of what it is they take themselves to be doing, or what they intend by doing something. We *could* simply say: "Clearly Ethan believes what he is doing in killing Debbie is saving her from the ignominy of spending her life as a squaw. He intends to do this and regards himself as justified in so acting because of some belief about the shamefulness of Indian life for a white girl and perhaps even because he believes the love of his life, Martha, would have wanted this." But all one need do is imagine how much of interest is drained from the film with such an explanation. The roles of revenge, self-hatred, Ethan's identification with Comanches, his self-deception, and the meaning of his reversal, among many other things, get no traction if we settle for such a flat-footed version of an adequate psychological explanation. Nothing of the dense layers of meaning in that famous look by Ethan remains if we settle this way.

This is all of course fairly messy psychologically and philosophically, and it greatly complicates the question of the possibility of an American politics. It being so messy is one of the reasons why what could be called political psychology is not among the prominent issues under discussion in contemporary political philosophy. (Liberal political philosophy has come to focus almost exclusively on the question of legitimacy.) If the issues are as described in *The Searchers*, then clearly the assessment and understanding of human motives and reasons in political situations of dependence and independence, of the weak and the powerful (which all greatly complicate any straightforward self-avowals and self-understanding), will require a subtlety, tentativeness, hermeneutical finesse, and exploratory approach that can be frustratingly incomplete and very difficult to deal with in theory. This is especially true in an age in which great promises are being made for the potential of a naturalist psychology, the neurosciences in particular, to unlock the mysteries of human conduct, human morality, and politics, and even for making great progress in understanding racism, criminality, sexism, and so forth. But for any such progress to be

made we need a way of individuating a person's standing attitudes and of identifying his effective motives, not merely his
avowed intentions. This is not even to begin to deal with the
problem of appropriate act-description and description of consequences within some community of assessment.

This messiness prompts another, dangerous temptation. By
dangerous I mean that some common forms of "character judgments" or other forms of holism in everyday explanations of action are quite close to the typology at work in the film's treatment
of racism: views about white, Indian, mixed blood, Texican, and
so forth. Ford is most certainly making use of the John Wayne
Type to "set up" the viewer, inducing an identification that Ford
will completely undermine by relying on our understanding of
that type, as if we know who "John Wayne" is, or for that matter as
if we know what America is. One element of the enormous emotional power of that famous scene of transformation and redemption is the realization that none of these archetypes is adequate to
the sudden, transformative gesture of Ethan picking up Debbie,
nor does it help us understand well the bitter, racist outburst of
Laurie, who had been such a faintly comic and pleasant character.

In fact this technique—the invitation to an identification
which is then frustrated, undermined, or in some way turned
against the identifier—is both a frequent device in the film and
often overlooked. I have just noted that Ford is inviting us at the
beginning of the film to take Ethan as *the* John Wayne Type, an
immensely competent, tough loner of great integrity and heroic

Plate 1

Plate 2

Plate 3

Plate 4

Plate 5

Plate 6

Plate 7

Plate 8

Plate 9

Plate 10

Plate 11

Plate 12

Plate 13

Plate 14

capacity. This assumption is so strong that I would venture to guess that perhaps most of the film's viewers simply glide over the fact that Ethan is a vicious racist, and are able to keep ignoring this until he finally rescues Debbie and this presumption about his "basically good and heroic" character seems finally confirmed. Likewise, we seemed to be invited into the jocular, racist hilarity enjoyed by Ethan when Martin marries Look, only to be shocked (and, one hopes, ashamed) when Martin brutally kicks her down a steep hill, and when we discover her massacred by white soldiers. And in an equally dangerous and tricky episode (for Ford), we are invited to apply the crudest of stereotypes when Ethan must pay for information from Futterman, clearly a Jewish trader, who has information about Debbie. We think that the stereotype about moneygrubbing and treacherousness is confirmed when Futterman and some confederates sneak into Ethan and Martin's camp and try to kill and rob them. But we then find that Ethan was willing to use a sleeping Martin as bait in an extremely risky trap, that he shoots all three robbers in the back, and that he rifles through Futterman's pockets and "steals" back his money. It is Ethan who turns out to be avaricious and treacherous.

VII

It is also clear just how complicated Ford's treatment of this is when we look at the last scene (fig. 4.14; plate 14), the fourth and

4.14

final use of the "inside-outside" shot in the film. I agree with those who argue that the shots help thematize the issue of who belongs to the civil community and who does not. That is, one could say that what the searchers have been searching for is not just Debbie, but "home," or even the meaning of home, kinship, some form of belonging together.[22] And it does at first glance look as if Ethan represents an archaic, even primitive reliance on race, blood, and ethnicity to establish such a home, and Martin seems the "modern" or even "American" hope—that race and ethnicity might eventually fade as markers of community. He is the product of intermarriage who will also intermarry; while Ethan's primitivism is banned and left outside.

But I also think that something much more complicated is going on. In the first place, there is another possible interpretation of the fact that there is no reconciliation scene with Ethan, that Ford took out the one that was in the shooting script.

The last scene could suggest that Ethan cannot come in because he knows that the reconciliation scene the Jorgensen's are enacting, the aspiration embodied in Martin, is, while not a complete fantasy, much more fragile than those "inside" are prepared to admit. (Throughout the film Ethan has taken on the role of protecting other characters from seeing something— Martin from seeing Martha, Martin and Brad from seeing Lucy, Martin from entering Scar's tent. He even tries to stop Mrs. Jorgensen from seeing the fight over her daughter. In this case too, he will simply leave them to their aspirations.) It is, after all, Ethan who stands in the light and the community who retreats to darkness, a complete and somewhat unnerving darkness when the door shuts.[23] I do not mean that Ethan is simply right about the fragility of conventional or constructed rather than "natural" political identity, or that he has achieved any genuine self-knowledge. He is still blind in many ways and so still must wander, as he does in the last shot we have of him, as if broken and newly burdened by what he has been through. But much of what he actually believes and is willing to do has been illuminated in the public world of action, has been exposed, and that is not true of the darkness inside (the community's self-understanding has not been tested like Ethan's, and he sometimes seems to be trying to help them prevent such a testing). The contrasting light and dark places can stand at least as a warning by Ford not to take for granted the overcoming of racism like Ethan's or Laurie's. (At the beginning of the film, Ford's camera lead us from the darkness into the light. At the end we retreat from the light into darkness.)

Put another way, with this last inside-out shot Ford is also thematizing something much more speculative—both the relation between the "inside" of a psyche and its outside, the observable, public bodily movements that constitute action and the great difficulties in understanding this connection. At the beginning of the film we have no reason to suspect any disconnect between what characters avow and what they do, and the transition from inside to outside is seamless and unproblematic. The family moves outside and welcomes Ethan; he moves inside and accepts the welcome. In the scene where Martha's body is discovered Ethan can be said to start his own journey into the darkest recesses of his heart, his "inside," the formation of what he takes to be his obligation for revenge and the murder of Debbie. (It is dark because his avowals and expressions of commitment and real desires are not transparent and not straightforwardly accessible to him. It is the beginning of a kind of insane resolve that will be manifest in the world, but not wholly, or not, finally, wholeheartedly, one might say, not in a way he can finally take responsibility for.) It is also from that perspective, from "inside Ethan," as if inside the frame of the experience for him, that we view the action from inside the cave as he rides Debbie down, and, given the way he calls her name, we understand "from his point of view" that he cannot kill her. In this sense, the withdrawal of the community back into the dark interior in this final scene suggests that we will be left with this gap between interior and exterior, with a self-understanding that cannot be made external or public because it is so self-deceived and content.

So while we are encouraged to believe that Ethan's racist pathology has no place in the "civilized world" and so is somehow rejected, two other issues stand out. We already know that Laurie shares the goals of Ethan's mad quest, and she certainly has not been redeemed, even though, to add to the complexity, she is to marry a "one-eighth" Indian. So the comforting geography of the last scene, a safe, civilized inside and an excluded, violent outside, is a lie; one, I would again venture to guess, the audience is all too happy to accept and that Ford is deliberately ironizing. (The interiors, again, are dark, as dark or opaque as the characters' self-knowledge. And we tend to forget that only Ethan could have rescued Debbie. Apart from Martin, the rest of them wanted to forget about her capture.) Second, the community does not reject Ethan. They rather ceremoniously ignore him. They pretend he does not exist; no one speaks to him, says goodbye, tells him he can or cannot come in. He is instantly forgotten, as if literally invisible. I take this as Ford's indicating some aspect of their own willful ignorance of their own racism (or their blindness, to go back to that theme: "Ain't got no eyes, can't enter the spirit land"), and their own (unacknowledged) need for a character like Ethan.

What might all this say about the American imaginary, if anything? I am sure that the character of Ethan, as the inheritor of the legacy of Natty Bumppo, Ahab, Sutpen and the like, is meant to raise that issue, but those questions are quite complicated. More obvious is his unusual treatment of the smugness and complacency and blindness of the white civilized world. Again, as noted before, perhaps the most shocking scene in the movie, in other words, is not Ethan's shooting the eyes out of a dead Indian or slaughtering buffaloes or trying to shoot Debbie or scalping Scar, but that little scene at Laurie's aborted wedding when she says:

> Fetch what home? The leavings of Comanche bucks, sold time and again to the highest bidder, with savage brats of her own? Do you know what Ethan will do if he has a chance? He'll put a bullet in her brain! I tell you Martha would want it that way.

5 CONCLUSION

I

IHAVE suggested that the great Hollywood Westerns present in a recognizably mythic form dimensions of an American self-understanding of great relevance to the question of the nature of the political in the American imaginary. They especially illuminate aspects of a distinct political psychology essential to the question of the use and acceptance of political power in modernity, aspects often neglected in narrower reflections on legitimacy in the liberal democratic philosophical tradition and more easily accessible in imaginative works of art. Many of these issues have to do with the kind of psychological stake that citizens are shown to have in private domestic life, and the relation between such a stake and a commitment to modern forms of political life. I also wanted to suggest that such movies in many instances embody and present not just such a mythical self-understanding. In ways that are technically subtle and somewhat elusive, some films also embody a kind of reflection about such mythological and epic self-understanding, and occasionally sound a kind of warning. Sometimes this warning is about the psychological insufficiencies of commercial republics when contrasted with depictions of older forms of virtue, the inability of such societies to sustain a deep allegiance, inspire heroic sacrifice, or allow for any significant form of satisfying mutual respect. Sometimes the situation is even more complicated, and it is the idealizations in the mythic narrative (themselves some sort of compensation for the absence of a long, common historical tradition) which themselves, in a regressive way, prevent a view of a more sober, realistic, pacific, and reconciled modern secular life. In this self-reflective, somewhat modernist moment some films can even be said to be about the "end of the Western" itself, the waning power of these narrative myths in our collective imaginary, the growing irrelevance, even if continued grip, of such stories in our political self-image. Sometimes this declining appeal is clearly being lamented, sometimes welcomed, often both.

A popular form of such Westerns concerns the aging gunfighter (someone who has outlived his time and role in history and so who is "untimely" in Nietzsche's sense, lost in the wrong historical epoch) or the gunfighter or "town-taming" lawman tired of being a gunfighter or such a lawman, trying to hang up his six-guns to become a "normal" person. Probably the most well-known version of the former is Don Siegel's 1976 movie starring John Wayne in his last role, *The Shootist*.[1] (Wayne had gotten used to playing this old-timer type since *True Grit* in 1969 and was cast to such a type in forgettable films like *Chisum* and *Big Jake* and *The Cowboys* and the truly awful *Cahill: U.S. Marshal*. He had a more respectable turn in *Rooster Cogburn* in 1975.) The most widely admired are probably Sam Peckinpah's *Ride the High Country* and *The Wild Bunch*. The latter genre, the "gunfighter who wants to quit" story, includes some very fine films: George Stevens's *Shane* is probably the most well known, but Anthony Mann's *Man of the West*, and Henry King's *Gunfighter* are also exemplars.

For our purposes, the framework of such narratives usually suggests that the transition situations that we have discussed are now over, the embourgeoisement of a new society pretty much complete, and so we get a double perspective on the ex-gunfighter. (As Gilberto Perez points out, many Westerns, especially Ford's, "look back to a past that looked forward to a future." The civil societies at issue in such Westerns are "open and unfinished,"[2] and so any so-called nostalgia is for a time when possibilities were open, not for any prefounding fixed way of cowboy life— like the dramatic unfinished church that is the setting for what is perhaps the single most beautiful image in Hollywood Westerns, the hesitant and awkward dance between Wyatt Earp [Henry Fonda] and Clementine [Cathy Downs] at that frame of a "possible" church in *My Darling Clementine* [figs. 5.1 and 5.2]. But there are also Westerns about the end of such possibility

5.1

5.2

and the beginning of routine and normalcy.)[3] When shown the
gunfighter's point of view, the viewer sees and experiences almost always a deep fatigue and world-weariness as a result of
the endless cycles of prefounding lawlessness, and so an idealization (from this point of view) of the pacific virtues of such a
finally settled domestic life. Shane is greatly attracted to the

Starrett family he is staying with precisely because it is a family, because he experiences the reality of familial love, especially the pleasures of a child. Gary Cooper's character in *Man of the West*, Link Jones, is happy enough to be his very small town's representative in its search for a schoolteacher and is profoundly unsettled when he suddenly must confront his outlaw past. (Jones himself, like many such characters, seems to embody the simple claim that there can *be* such a transition, that violence and disorder can be tamed and "left behind." Accordingly his gradual and then stunning transformation back into the killer he was, even if now for the sake of the good, is unsettling beyond the issue of his particular psychology.) In *The Gunfighter*, Gregory Peck's weary character, Jimmy Ringo, wants in some way to travel back in time, to revisit the romantic love and family (a child) that his wild life led him from. But what is striking about these plots is that in many cases the gunfighter or ex-outlaw or ex-frontier lawman *cannot* quit, is not "allowed" to leave the life he had led. That is, the idealization of the settled domestic life that he wants to join turns out to be far too idealistic, his stark division between his pre-legal, violent, and wild outlaw or gunfighter life and a modern law-and-order, peaceful society and domestic bliss is far too stark. What he finds when he begins to live among the law-abiding and churchgoing is, to his great consternation, a profound need *for him*, for his skill in the ways of violence. There is usually a crisis brewing, and the sheriff or marshal or all the townsfolk are not up to the task. A "state of

exception" always looms. When the plots suggest that the gunfighter cannot outlive or outrun his past, that character is destiny, this often is also because there are violent and outlaw
elements everywhere *within* the supposedly peaceful world he
wants to slip back into; often it is a younger version of himself
out to make his mark. (As with *Red River,* we meet transitions
that are not really transformations. Tom cannot outrun his past
or his destiny any more than the community can rightly claim
to have transcended and overcome the law of the gun.) This
somewhat ironic twist—that the domestic world of commercial
republics itself still contains, still relies on, must still deal with,
but in many ways hides from itself, elements of disorder, injus-
tice, and violence that the gunfighter is trying to escape and
that only someone like him can cope with—"completes" the
Western narrative of founding and law in a way that itself seems
to embody the weariness, disappointment, and final, stoic resig-
nation of the gunfighter himself.

On the other hand, in some films, from the perspective of
the community or the new settled world, the gunfighter or ex-
outlaw is understood not only as a man, as it were, from "out of
the past,"[4] but as a theatrical or commercial object, unreal, or
the stuff of *commercial* myth and legend, not the new modern
reality the community believes itself to live in. This obviously
creates some tension. The illusion of a full transition from the
"frontier" and all that that has come to signify is just that—an
illusion—but the hiddenness and subtlety and to some extent

internalized nature of bourgeois violence allow the luxury of a common representation of the frontier as overcome. The figure for such a purported "dead and gone" past, for this illusory self-representation, is the theatrical cowboy. Such films in effect show us the process of the theatricalization of such a character and such a self-image, no longer a historical actuality or a mythologically alive historical memory. This is of course something the Western film itself also participates in, and the figure for the film's own role in both presenting the mythic image and plot and the transformation of such a past into theatrical elements is often a pulp fiction writer who scurries along after the aging hero, eager to provide his readers with a vicarious look at how it was (or who wants to be there when the hero finally dies). Often the presentation of what the Western, or such a mythic self-understanding, has become in the new commercial world shows it to be tawdry, even pathetic, a theatricalized echo of what it was, on view and of interest but no longer functioning as part of an actual mythic self-consciousness; rather on parade as a commercial object for mere entertainment. (The reflexive relation of such a stance to the Hollywood film is often intended.)

There is an interesting treatment of such themes in a film that its director insisted was not a Western, although he might very well have meant that its not being a Western, its not being able to be a Western, is the whole point of the movie.[5] (For one thing, nothing of public or political significance hangs on the resolution of the plot, but that absence is very much part of the

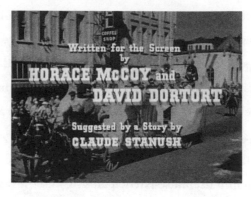

5.3

5.4

story too. The bourgeois family figures a nonpolitical haven in a way that suggests something about the ideals of the bourgeois world itself and their relatively non-political fate.)[6] And it begins with a "Western" parade (figs. 5.3 and 5.4). I mean *The Lusty Men,* directed by Nicholas Ray (1952), an interesting variation on the aging gunfighter theme, and I would like to address its treatment of the "end of the Western," or the "theatricalization of the Western myth."[7] This transformation of the national self-understanding typical of Westerns into a theatricalized show is quite explicit in the film: it is a rodeo movie, the rodeo being the modern inheritor of the Wild West show tradition. What were once real skills necessary in the real West, skill in horseback riding, bronco busting, roping, and marksmanship, are now on display in essentially meaningless if still dangerous competitions.[8] But even within this theatricalized framework Ray introduces an essential dimension of the underlying psychological drama in so many Westerns.

At the center of the story is an aging (he is supposed to be around thirty-five) former world champion rodeo star, Jeff McCloud, played in a beautifully understated performance by Robert Mitchum. The film opens with him bucked off a Brahma bull for what seems like the last time. He walks out of the empty arena (through the "Stock Exit"), alone and in a somewhat desolate setting and, apparently since he is in the area, he hitches a ride to his nearby boyhood home. He meets unexpectedly the present owner, who asks him what he is doing snooping around, and Jeff replies, "I was looking for something I thought I had lost" (a kind of leitmotif of many Westerns). Through Jeff we are introduced to a number of "updated" Western themes. The life of an itinerant rodeo performer does duty for the wandering gunfighter or cowboy, outside of society, living the Western equivalent of a bohemian life (gambling, drinking, rodeo groupies, and so forth, enjoying what Jeff describes as a "different kind of buzz"), and like the aging gunfighter, yearning now for home ("something I thought I had lost"). In fact the issue of home, and its modern American version in the nuclear family, owning a small piece of something, *private* property and a private life, soon become the center of the movie.

For Jeff meets Wes Merritt and his wife, Louise (Arthur Kennedy and Susan Hayward). Wes is a cowhand on a nearby ranch, and the Merritts have their eye on the small ranch where Jeff grew up. But they must scrape and save, and Wes is clearly losing patience. He is starstruck by the famous Jeff McCloud, and is a pretty good amateur rodeo rider himself. To the great consternation of his wife, Wes begins to enter rodeos and to win with Jeff as his teacher and partner (sharing Wes's winnings), and soon the three of them are traveling around, doing quite well. The film thus sets up an explicit contrast and some tension between a life outside the conventions of a normal modern American domestic life on the one hand (something Ray conventionally associates with the woman, Louise), and a wilder, less regulated, risky, and hyper-masculine life, what is left of the Wild West life, however tinged with pathos. This sort of tension then breaks out explicitly in the Merritts' marriage. Wes is getting a big head; he enjoys the winning, the lifestyle, and, increasingly, the groupies; he forgets that such a life can only be temporary. Louise finally tells him that when she married him "you weren't the biggest, you weren't the strongest, the richest or

the prettiest, but you're the one who wanted what I wanted."
And we know she means a home. (We learn that Louise's parents were migrant workers and that she grew up in tents, always
on the move.) The speech she makes is not exactly a romantic
one, and when she accuses Jeff of freeriding with them, of "latching on" to Wes's success, Jeff can easily turn the tables and ask,
"Who is latching onto who here?" (Louise had been working in a
tamale factory and was ferociously committed to getting out of
that world.)

In films like *My Darling Clementine* this promise of a settled,
peaceful domestic life, the end of the Wild West, can be treated
as a kind of dream, a goal that is easy to fantasize about when
caught up in the world of the Clampetts. (The unfinished church
in Tombstone has no name and not even yet a preacher. As with
the ending of many Westerns, it is an expression of hope.) In
films like *The Man Who Shot Liberty Valance*, when the promise
is realized something vital seems to have gone missing, and so
the heroization of Ranse Stoddard seems required. In Delmar
Daves's *3:10 to Yuma*, the inglorious life of a small farmer prompts
a kind of shame before his boy at the smallness and banality of
such a life, and so prompts a wild risk (which the outlaw appreciates and even himself sacrifices for). In many of the films of Budd
Boetticher the issue is handled as a question about the fate of
"masculinity" in such societies. In the many "feudal baron" or
"private empire" movies (such as *Man from Laramie, The Furies,
The Big Country, Forty Guns,* and *Duel in the Sun*), the grandeur,

power, and beauty of such a form of life is contrasted with "dirt farmers" and "sheepherders" and merely commercial (and so venal) interests like the railroad. The issue comes up often in Westerns and is handled in all sorts of ways. It is the question we have raised in a number of contexts; let us say it is the question of the psychological sufficiency of modern American domestic existence and so the political ramifications of such a psychological reality. But here in *The Lusty Men* we know exactly what is supposed to somehow reestablish some grip on Wes's imagination and draw him back. It is the contemporary settled bourgeois life most of us know and that we see at the peaceful dinner that Jeff enjoys with the Merritts at the beginning of the film. And the rodeo theme helps emphasize that the virtues of a supposedly more independent or authentic or more intense life are (or have now become) phony, existing only in a theatricalized and now largely irrelevant reenactment of the Western life.

But what is so unusual about the treatment here is the way Louise gets Wes back (and the fact that Ray so intelligently, without anything maudlin or sentimental, manifests such deep sympathy with this hope for a home). At a big fracas at a party, Wes had refused to leave with Louise, and he called out Jeff, accusing him of freeloading and of being a coward. Jeff declares his love to Louise when he starts to take her home, and she rejects him, but again not for any very romantic reasons. She wants her life with Wes, she says, that home, that family—and that is all she wants. (She wants, that is, the marriage and domestic life that had been the object of such attention and such great skepticism in the novels of Flaubert and Tolstoy, Fitzgerald and Roth.) She knows she is not likely to get that from Jeff, so she asks his help in getting Wes back. She gets it, but in a remarkable way.

Jeff signs up the next day for all the dangerous events in the rodeo, and there are all sorts of indirect hints that this is especially dangerous for him, given all his injuries. He falls and is badly injured. They carry him off on a stretcher, and in the first-aid area, in a remarkably subtle and underplayed scene, an extraordinary event occurs. We get the impression that Jeff has done all this for Louise to show Wes the folly of continuing on the rodeo circuit (of indulging the fantasies about an independent and wilder life) and so to shock some sense into him. We hear the doctor caution Jeff to lie very still, and he tells him that he has broken a rib and punctured a lung. But instead of lying still he rolls awkwardly and forcefully onto his left side, seems to embrace Louise and thereby, we infer, punctures his heart too, or at least deliberately causes a mortal internal wound, and he dies (fig. 5.5). This has the desired effect on Wes, who is stunned back into the domestic world Louise wants, and they walk off through the exit sign (the one for people this time), destined for the ranch they had wanted to buy.

I have mentioned several times how the difficult problem of "vainglory" or pride and honor plays an important role in so many Westerns. In Ray's film, such glory is sacrificed and in true melodramatic form—in an unknown or virtually unknown

5.5

sacrifice. Jeff gives up everything for Louise and for what Louise
wants, a home. With the way that gesture is treated (given Ray's
mise-en-scène, as the *Cahiers* critics would put it) there is a kind
of affirmation by Ray that Jeff's sacrifice was worth it, that
there is nothing petty or small-minded or cowardly about what
Louise wants. It is worth wanting; it is especially worth giving
up what Wes has been chasing, what has become a mere com-
mercialized simulacrum of the Western self-image. It is what
the various foundings depicted by Westerns were *for*, and so it is
worth what so many films suggest must be sacrificed to achieve:
vainglory, a putative radical independence and self-reliance, supposedly masculine virtues, an honor code. It is a theme one often sees in Ford, but, as noted, Ford deals only with the idealized
promise of such a future, and one might see this last gesture as
Ray's confirmation that Ford was right. Most great Westerns,
that is, are about the end of the way of life pictured and some-

times glorified in film, and while the transitions they depict can be confusing, multidimensional, and hard to assess, there are few documents of American self-understanding in which the issues are posed in a more gripping and compelling way than in Westerns or in "end of the Western" films like Nicholas Ray's *The Lusty Men.*

NOTES

Chapter 1. Introduction

1. The exception is Peacock, the whiskey salesman, who keeps reasonably protesting that the crossing is much too dangerous. He is the only one, we might say, whose fate is determined by the "force" of the common or democratic will of the group. He even seems to understand this and, while protesting, to sign on to the fate that they have come to share.

2. Tocqueville (1969), p. 57.

3. See Rothman (2003), p. 161.

4. See the remarks below on Frederick Jackson Turner. This is hardly the end of the story. The tension in the American desire for the eventual refinement of civilized life and the fact that such refinement was not possible without reintroducing a social hierarchy, and one which was often portrayed in Westerns as enervated and potentially corrupt and hypocritical, is portrayed in many Westerns (*My Darling Clementine* is an interesting case) and has been much discussed. See especially Henry Nash Smith (2005), p. 215; and with regard to *Stagecoach*, Gallagher (1986), p. 161; Wood (1971), pp. 31–32; Grant (2001) on Natty Bumppo, Cooper, and Ford, pp. 207ff; and Studlar (2003), p. 145.

5. See Rothman (2003), p. 159. Perez (1998) suggests that Ringo knows, and he notes that, when Dallas asked Ringo to give up his revenge quest and go off with her, he had, contrary to many stereotypes of Ford and Westerns, *agreed* (hardly the "masculinist" answer). It is also important that Lucy's baby is a girl. Cf. pp. 238–39. This issue of the relation between self-sufficient independence and domestic dependence will surface frequently in the discussion below.

6. See the contrasting accounts of Browne (1975), pp. 26–38, and Gallagher (1986), pp. 153–60, and Rothman's summation (2003), pp. 174–76.

7. Politics involves violence and coercion, but if you can be shown, "in principle," perhaps by some quite complex argument, to be coercing yourself, then you have no genuine complaint about being coerced, even if you think you do. As Dworkin (2000) has put it, you can have no "complaint in liberty" when you are prohibited from doing something you are not entitled to do. So there can be no conflict between liberty and any other genuine value. For a counter (with which I agree), see Williams (2005), p. 84.

8. Others, like Carl Schmitt, think that the political dimension in human life must always involve the highest possible stakes for one's group or community, the possibility or actuality of an enemy, and is truly visible only in war (or civil war) or in anticipation of war.

9. Rousseau (1986), p. 22.

10. John Ford's *Man Who Shot Liberty Valance* depicts precisely this problem. A man who is always morally certain of the right thing to do must come to terms with the fact that the rule of law often not only permits but actually requires what such law would also prohibit.

11. Rawls (1971), p. 454. Whether Rawls is true to this condition or not is a subject for much debate and, given the direction of Rawls's later work, was obviously an issue for him as well.

12. Of course, the long debate in modern social theory about an "understanding" (*Verstehen*) versus an "explanation" (*Erklären*) model of account-giving is relevant to this topic. There is no time to wander into that forest, but I shall simply assume that something crucial in our account of human life is missing if we leave out the question "What it is like to be a political subject?" or the "participant" point of view, and that this question cannot be answered from the "spectator" point of view.

13. I shall assume here that the battle over the issue of whether "Hollywood movies" merit close, sustained attention as serious works of art (and not merely as revealing artifacts of use for sociology, history, or anthropology) has been settled on the side of Hollywood, and that one can hold such a view without being committed to any particular version of auteur theory, and without a commitment to any particular film theory. It should be sufficient to cite the work of Stanley Cavell to establish that (or such fine books as Perez [1998] or Wilson [1986]). For a compelling book-length defense, see Perkins (1993).

14. Bazin (1971a) and Warshow (1998). See also Bazin (1971b). Warshow does not talk explicitly in terms of myth, but his essay is all about "patterns," "structure," and "codes."

15. There are various ways of counting such plots. The most prevalent are probably (i) the ex-gunfighter trying to find a way to quit, which is in tension with the town's need for his violent skills, or the general travails of ex-gunfighters who have simply become irrelevant; (ii) the empire-ranch story, in which a kind of feudal lord holds power threatened by the coming of civilization and the dissolution of the next generation; (iii) episodes in the Indian wars, especially journeys across hostile territory; (iv) captivity narratives; (v) free-range ranchers trying to stop homesteaders and farmers from putting up fences and establishing claims to land; (vi) revenge quests; and (vii) wagon train movies, in which colonizers are out to stake claims farther west. Cf. Kitses's "antinomies" series in Kitses

(1969), p. 11, and Frank Gruber's list of seven plot types, cited in Cawelti (1971), p. 40.

16. Some think that the prototypical early fictional Western, Owen Wister's *The Virginian*, simply transposed the Knights of the Round Table into the American West, with cowboys as knights and the tyrannical owners of vast private cattle empires as kings and their families as royal families. It is certainly true that *The Virginian* contributed what would become staples of narrative in Westerns, of all sorts, summarized by Perez (1988): "the fallible friend, the schoolteacher from the East, the climactic shootout with the villain on the main street of the town" (p. 236). See Böhringer (1998), p. 9, and Bayertz on the "Klassizität" of Westerns (1981), p. 138, and his comparison of Westerns with the other national epics mentioned here (2003), p. 74. The Lancelot-Guinevere issue certainly plays a part in *Shane, The Searchers, The Man Who Shot Liberty Valence, Seven Men from Now,* and many B Westerns, such as *Man in the Saddle.*

17. I mean to appeal to the notion of myth as broadly as did Bazin, and I have no particular ax to grind in the debates about structuralist, psychoanalytic, and various comparativist methodologies. I have found helpful the Introduction to Maranda (1972); chapter 2 (on Levi-Strauss) and chapter 5 in Kirk (1970); the essay by Leach ("Myth as a Justification for Faction and Social Change") in George (1968), pp. 184–98; and several essays in Middleton (1967). I am grateful to my colleague Paul Friedrich for discussing these issues in modern anthropology and their relevance to Westerns.

18. Tomins (1992) is the most well-known critic of Westerns on this issue. (She argues that Westerns are about "men's fear of losing their mastery, and hence their identity" [p. 45], and she sees this as part of a cultural struggle against what had become the dominance of the feminine sentimental novel in the nineteenth century.) I agree with Perez (1988) that she misses the "politics of the Western" (p. 251) or interprets all politics in the Western as sexual politics.

19. Cawelti (1971), p. 38.

20. The details of Turner's claim have been heavily criticized, especially his pretense that the "savage" and the "civilized" can be so sharply distinguished. (Herbert Eugene Bolton's contrasting notion of "borderlands" and a greater suspicion about traditional assumptions concerning the "units" of historical analysis are much more prominent today.) See also Smith (2005) and the very different, somewhat mystical account of violence in Slotkin (1973), (1998). (All I need from Turner is the relevance of the idea of first an "open" and then a "closed" or closing frontier in the American imaginary, in its shared view of itself as a nation, however subject to some self-deceit is that image. The limitations of such a mythic self-understanding are actually often on view and thematized as such *in* Westerns, as we will see).

21. The great Italian director of Westerns, Sergio Leone, said it well: "The first reaction to the great fury of Achilles is the stunned silence of everyone present. The entrance of the killer into the saloon works the same way. The piano player stops playing, and everyone is struck dumb, as if pillars of salt."

22. To some extent this is what distinguishes them from the almost wholly mythic, nearly placeless, wholly typological, largely ahistorical Italian Westerns of Sergio Leone.

23. Perez (1988), p. 237.

24. This point is made in a different way by Smith (2005), p. 223. See also, with reference to the Turner thesis, p. 255.

25. Even politicians in the 1960s could call up an imaginary "new frontier" and keep the image alive.

26. See the interesting essay by Studlar (2003), who also connects these original social pressures with the Great Depression.

27. Hegel (1969), Bd. 12, p. 113. Früchtl's discussion, pp. 37–44 is very helpful on these points.

28. While the first great Western was made in 1939 (*Stagecoach*), the heyday was clearly the fifties and there is lots to say about the

relation between Westerns and that particular audience for Westerns. It also means that the topic calls up a generational divide. Childhoods of my generation were dominated by the television characters Roy Rogers and Gene Autry and the Cisco Kid, and Zorro and the Lone Ranger, and shows like *Rawhide*, and *Wagon Train*, and *Gunsmoke*, and *The Rifleman*, and *Have Gun, Will Travel* (my favorite), and *Wanted: Dead or Alive*, and even *Bonanza* (which I hated). I doubt that many of my students had Daniel Boone coonskin caps and fake Davie Crockett Bowie knives (I did) or received cowboy outfits and toy pistols for Christmas, or spent all day Saturdays at the movies (10 in the morning until 6 at night), watching one Western after another.

29. Hirschman (1977).

Chapter 2. *Red River* and the Right to Rule

1. See the account in Jung and Kerényi (1949) in the section "The Special Phenomenology of the Child Archetype," pp. 86ff.

2. Stopping at Abilene instead of continuing to Kansas City cuts off 160 miles or so, an enormous saving in time and wear and tear on the cattle.

3. This is a theme dealt with marvelously by Kurosawa in *The Seven Samurai*.

4. Of course, herding cattle as an image of the political has another side to it, a suggestion of what mass politics has become: managing a herdlike conformist group of indistinguishable cows who nevertheless can explode into irrational fanaticism.

5. Tom's sermonizing about "good beef for hungry people" is one of many attempts by him to give his enterprise this broad ethical significance. There is precious little evidence that Dunson has given much thought to hungry people, however. What is exactly intended by Hawks in such cases is unclear and irrelevant anyway. There just is something bathetic about these self-congratulatory speeches.

6. Let me put the point in the terms used by Hegel in his *Lectures on Aesthetics*. According to Hegel, a mythic perspective and an epic narrative presuppose for the credibility of the narrative a specific (and old) form of historical life and a specific set of ethical presuppositions. The most important assumption is the centrality of the hero and the way an issue of universal significance—the fate of a nation and its values—rests on the actions of an individual (however venal some of his individual, actual motives might be). That sort of world is not ours; ours is an unheroic and prosaic world. But in Hegel's historical narration, the progress of human self-understanding is not like a train ride from point A to an end station B. In historical time, we might say that the past is more like geological layers that accumulate and still make their presence felt, still exert a kind of pressure on action and have some hold on our imagination. (They do not vanish once surpassed.) This means that in certain historical contexts it might very well be that an epic framework and a mythic point of view could render a situation more intelligible, could make clearer the ethical options available and relevant. Traveling West is like traveling backward in time too, so Tom Dunson's view of the way to understand the task they face and the role he is entitled to play might be right. We need to see how Hawks handles this issue.

7. A rebellious federation of states that, in effect, seceded from the British Empire will also face the problem of such consistency when some of those federated states themselves want to secede.

8. Many Westerns revolve around a pair of characters who seem to figure as two sides of the heroic character, or of any heroic character: a violent, extralegal, "elemental" side, and a domesticated, law-abiding side. A familiar version of this: the Prostitute and the Good Girl: Dallas and the pregnant army wife, Mrs. Mallory, in *Stagecoach;* Chihuahua and Clementine in *My Darling Clementine;* and especially Helen Ramirez (Katy Jurado) and Amy Kane (Grace Kelly) in *High Noon;* Doc Holliday and Wyatt Earp in *Clementine,*

too. Tom Dunafon and Ransom Stoddard in *The Man Who Shot Liberty Valance* are such a pair, as, one might argue, are Scar and Ethan in *The Searchers* (although this is much more complicated since they are also very close to the same type, as if Scar is more an emanation, in the Blakean sense, of Ethan), or Dunson and Matt here. Even better: Cherry Valance and Matt; the Dancing Kid and Johnny Guitar in *Johnny Guitar;* Kimbrough and Allison in *Decision at Sundown;* Morgan and Blaisdell in *Warlock;* Blaisdell and Gannon too in that film in an oddly symmetrical use of the theme. Perhaps the source for such narration goes back to Chingachgook and Natty Bumppo.

9. One of the great problems in empire Westerns, as in many mythic stories of royal fathers and their sons, is the problem of succession. The claim for a natural entitlement to rule, as if by force of charismatic authority, appeals to something like a natural right, but such a virtue, if it is a virtue, cannot be inherited; or at least it is obvious in almost all such stories that it cannot be. So there is often a corrupt "natural" son and a more suitable but nonfamilial adopted son, or there is a "bad" older son and a "good" but less brutal, more cultured younger son, as in King Vidor's 1946 *Duel in the Sun.* The best example, I think, is Anthony Mann's 1955 *Man from Laramie.* There is the beginning of this kind of plot in *Red River* in the ominous competition between Cherry and Matt, made more potentially intense because neither is natural heir, but for various reasons that element of the plot fizzles.

10. It has often been noted that Hawks seems to set up the antagonistic relation between Cherry and Matt, and so perhaps their roles as alternative visions of modern rule, only to let the issue evaporate, go unresolved. The usual explanation (offered by the scriptwriter, Borden Chase) is that John Ireland started fooling around with Hawks's girlfriend at the time, so a lot of the Cherry-Matt conflict was dropped in a fit of Hawksean pique. Hawks notes the rumor but denies it in McBride (1996), p. 149, claiming that the real

reason he was irritated with Ireland was because he got drunk and smoked marijuana every night, and so kept losing his hat and gun, wasting too much time on the set.

11. Hawks goes so far as to have Tess repeat the words of Fen about erotic passion, "My knees feel like they have knives in them." See Hawks's remarks in McBride (1996), p. 86.

12. For a different sort of "defense" of the ending, see Wood (2006), pp. 116–23.

13. See Bogdanovich (1962), p. 27. He also says that, given Wayne's character and Clift's character, "the only way they could end up was just the way they did." McBride (1996), p. 151.

14. One of the most interesting treatments of this theme—call it supreme bourgeois self-confidence—is William Wyler's 1958 *The Big Country*. McKay (Gregory Peck), with his faith in technology (he has a compass and can navigate vast distances alone) and his lack of any need to display his prowess (he learns to ride a powerful horse in secret) and his serene attitude toward the macho displays around him (he regards it all as infantile), can be seen as an even more developed version of Matt Garth and his confidence.

15. Cf. the interesting contrast between Hawks (usually quite skeptical about the values of civilization) and Ford ("cinema's great poet of civilization") by Wood (1971), p. 12.

16. There is another large mythological dimension relevant here. As in the Kronos-Zeus or Laius-Oedipus and Freudian archetype, the slaying and often mutilation of the father (Dunson is seriously "crippled" after all) is undertaken by the sons in envy and rage at the father's possession of the mother. But in *Red River*, an odd inversion occurs. The father in effect rejects, even can be said to sacrifice, the woman in some sense in favor of the son. The absence of women in the movie thus seems connected with the absence of true rebellion and so the more extensive, more subtle, more effective reign of the father-tyrant. I doubt whether Hawks intended this as a comment on the unusual status (nonstatus) of women in

America, as, say, Tocqueville did, but the theme is certainly there in the film.

17. If one were inclined in a Foucauldean direction, one could note here Matt's implicit insight that inspiring self-discipline and self-policing is much more effective than relying on Dunson's external, patriarchal authority.

18. This is actually a theme in all the Westerns I will discuss. All three involve a complex relationship between an older, severe man, and a younger, or at least psychologically younger (naïve) man: Tom and Matt in *Red River*, Tom and Ransome in *The Man Who Shot Liberty Valance*, and Ethan and Martin in *The Searchers*. And all three relationships raise a question central to modernity— whether the great potential violence and moral anarchy of nature and human nature can in fact be tamed, or whether we can get by, must get by, with only a comforting, mythologically created and sustained illusion that it can.

19. See Früchtl's discussion (2004), p. 90.

20. So the film ends as it began, with the question of writing, the question of who is writing what for whom and why, and so the question of who writes the relevant history.

Chapter 3. Who Cares Who Shot Liberty Valance?

1. And they often serve religious purposes of course. They help establish what is sacred, forbidden, commanded, and so forth.

2. These references to the function of myth-telling are not precise terms of art, and the difficulties one runs into in trying to account for them might quickly drive one back to the conventional view: that these movies are simply entertaining adventure stories. I am trying to make the case that this would be a mistake.

3. Walzer (1996), pp. 23ff.

4. Kallen (1924), pp. 51, 122. Cf. Walzer's discussion (1996), pp. 23 passim.

5. Rawls (1971), p. 527.

6. As it is put by Philip Gleason in the *Harvard Encyclopedia of American Ethnic Groups*, "A person does not have to be of any particular national, linguistic, religious or ethnic background. All he had to do was to commit himself to the political ideology centered on the abstract ideals of liberty, equality and republicanism" (Gleason [1980], p. 32. Quoted in Walzer [1996], p. 30).

7. Walzer's discussion (1996) is once again interesting on this point. He claims that the "ideals of citizenship do not today make a coherent whole" (p. 95) and that "patriotism" and "political activism" pull us one way and the implications of "civility and toleration" pull us toward a more passive political life. His most remarkable claim is that we have now just about the right level of active political participation: not very much. A more active public life would be more dangerous and divisive than we might have bargained for. (This seems a kind of revival of Madison's old worries about factionalism in democracies.) But with respect to our topic, he makes the following observation: "The new citizenship, however, leaves many Americans dissatisfied. Liberalism, even at its most permissive, is a hard politics because it offers so few emotional rewards; the liberal state is not a home for its citizens; it lacks warmth and intimacy. And so contemporary dissatisfaction takes the form of a yearning for political community, passionate affirmation, explicit patriotism. These are dangerous desires, for they cannot readily be met within the world of liberalism" (p. 96).

8. Another very good treatment of the general question of what form of political life is suitable for a bourgeois social order, and so how the relation between private and public should be understood, is André de Toth's 1959 *Day of the Outlaw*. The possibility that what is announced and avowed as a political motive could easily be understood as a violent personal passion is the major idea in the film. And the film goes further by showing how the realization of this duplicity can also radically alter one's sense of the importance of one's

private desires, how much and in what sense they should matter. There is a fine performance here too by Robert Ryan; he attempts to be cynical and world-weary and finds he cannot be.

9. Rousseau (1986), p. 199.

10. Weber (2002), p. 121.

11. Weber (1994), p. xvi.

12. Modern political philosophy—Locke's, for example—assumes a complicated and complexly formed social subject, hardly something one can take for granted. One imagines the early history of industrialization and the generations required to create subjects willing to work harder than is necessary to maintain the status quo into which they were born, and the great psychological costs of such a socialization. See Anthony (1977), pp. 22, 41; Hutt (1939), chapter 5. I was put onto these sources by the interesting discussion in Coetzee (1988), chapter 1.

13. Kahn (2004), p. 4

14. For a good account of the Dorothy Johnson novel on which the film is based, see Leutrat (1995), pp. 12ff, and see also Leutrat's discussion of Ford's adaptation, pp. 27ff.

15. If Andrew Sarris (1975) and his source are right, it is likely that the state is Colorado (p. 179). (In [1962] he had guessed Arizona or New Mexico.)

16. The film was criticized for the way Ford used much older actors to play much younger roles. (Stewart was fifty-three, and the young Ranse is clearly supposed to be in his late twenties. Vera Miles, who as the young Hallie may even be in her teens, was thirty-three!) McBride and Wilmington (1975) seem to suggest that this was partly deliberate on Ford's part, that he wanted to achieve the effect of older people projecting themselves back into the past, to make that fact visible on screen, rather than present the flashback as a return to the events themselves. That's a nice point. See their interesting discussion, pp. 175–89. Ford also drops an important but subtle hint that what we are about to be told, what will be seen in the

movie, is only a version of what happened. Things have been omitted. When Ranse begins talking with the young journalist he tells him that he (Ranse) will cooperate because "Dutton Peabody once fired me." There is no such episode in the flashback/film. On the contrary, Peabody and Stoddard are close allies. See Leutrat's discussion (1995), p. 65. And of course, as noted, in Ranse's version, we never see Tom and Hallie alone together. (Of course, this may just be a "continuity" oversight.)

17. See Perkins (1965) on the "contradiction" in the film's treatment of the old and new Shinbone. And Wood (1971) on the opening: "All vitality has drained away, leaving only the shallow energy of the news-hounds, and a weary, elegiac feeling of loss" (p. 9).

18. One only has a very slight visual cue as a basis for any inference about this all-important issue. (Does Hallie know the true story?)

19. His Vince Stone character in Fritz Lang's *Big Heat* is a worthy contender for such a title.

20. The equation of a more civilized order, the rule of law, and the domestic virtues with femininity is a complex notion at work in all three films and a prominent topic in early modern political philosophy. Note that even the tough-minded Hobbes believes that, in the language of these films (most of which, I am trying to suggest, is ironic), civilized order, in the traditional gendered categories, feminizes us all, persuading us to lay down our arms, give up the pursuit of vainglory, value security and peace above all else, and create a Leviathan state. See the brilliant discussion by Victoria Kahn in (2004). Kahn rightly notes that this means that the main question at issue in Hobbes's picture is not so much the rationality of the contract that brings the Leviathan into being, but the psychological sufficiency of his account of human motivation.

21. Gallagher's discussion (1986), pp. 408ff, is especially helpful on these points.

22. The proximate event that kicks off the duel is also quite relevant—a vicious beating administered to Peabody, the newspaper

man, by Valance. In one sense, this reminds us that, of all the characters, Peabody is the only character whose psychological motives are straightforwardly political, are not in any way we can see entangled in erotic rivalry, personal honor, or intimate friendships. He simply believes in a free press and in democracy, and in his drunken, bombastic way, is one of the most heroic figures in the movie.

23. Even though by present standards he is certainly also patronizing and infantilizing. ("You're pretty when you're mad," and so forth.)

24. Cf. Bordwell's remarks (1971), p. 19.

25. For a penetrating discussion of how the film approaches revolutionary violence, see Brunkhorst (2006).

26. My thanks to Victor Perkins for his comments about these scenes. Perhaps the most moving treatment of this theme—the yearning for a "home" in a world that is generally more and more homeless—is Nicholas Ray's very fine *The Lusty Men*. See chapter 5.

27. Cf. Leutrat (1995), "La légende et les faits constituent un dispositif à tiroirs; tous s'alignent et la distinction s'estompe sans que l'on sache où sont les faits."

28. Captain York (Wayne) knows that Colonel Thursday is a martinet, an egomaniac, a racist, and a bad commander who needlessly got his troops killed. But at the end of the movie, York indulges in a grotesque glorification of "Thursday's charge" and has clearly himself (as the new commander) taken on the imperialist and heartless task of defeating the Indians (with whom, we have been shown, he has much sympathy). Given what Ford has shown us about Thursday (no aspect of whom is redeemed by any positive quality) I think Ford means this to be deeply troubling and tragic, but many who see the film seem to believe that Ford is insisting that such a lie and such blindness to the human costs of the empire are all necessary or even good. I don't know what to say at such a point except see more Ford movies.

29. Obviously the Shinbone incidents are not historical events, so we are not being disabused by the film of any historical myths of our own, but the lesson seems to be that myths and legends are always different from facts, that we usually need to ignore this, and are "now" in a position (apparently) to deal only with the facts.

30. Impossible, although Slotkin seems to think that films like Fort Apache do encourage such a strange doxastic state. Slotkin (1998), p. 342.

31. One could argue that Ford in this film stacks the deck a bit for the viewer. There are none of the typical Monument Valley vistas in the film and surprisingly few outside shots at all—the railroad scenes and Tom's ranch, but not much else. It is a much more domestic, "inside" film than other Ford Westerns. Accordingly, we don't get as forcefully the suspicion here that we sometimes do (by contrast) that "nature," in its majesty, beauty, and power, hardly needs human "improvement," that attempts to harness or master it are both presumptuous and pathetic. Nevertheless, the mere device of the cactus rose, what Hallie had been asked to give up for a "real rose," still helps suggest that the question she asks sounds with a touch of irony and emptiness.

32. See the helpful discussion by Koch (2006), especially her note that Hallie's reaction to Tom's death and Ranse's stupefied response remind one of Joyce's story *The Dead*, in which a husband learns of his wife's burning love for someone else.

33. I don't want to seem too hard on Stoddard. Brunkhorst (2006) makes a good point when he notes that Ransom also seems, self-consciously, to take on the role of sacrificial victim (another familiar mythological element [Moses could not reach the Promised Land]), that he will have to live with his lie, just as Tom must with his murder, for the greater good. This willingness first manifests itself, as Brunkhorst notes, in the confrontation between Tom and Liberty in the restaurant. They are about to kill each other over who will pick up Tom's steak, and Ransom intervenes and picks up

the steak, offering himself, as his name suggests, as ransom. This is clearly a foreshadowing of Ransom's role in the duel later.

34. "The truth is that the Westerner comes into the field of serious art only when his moral code, without ceasing to be compelling, is seen also to be imperfect. The Westerner at his best exhibits a moral ambiguity which darkens his image and saves him from absurdity; this ambiguity arises from the fact that, whatever his justifications, he is a killer of men." Warshow (1998), p. 39.

35. See Koch's remarks on such truth and Arendt (2006).

36. Ford's perspective on this issue is vast and distinctive. Sarris (1962) sums it all up very well. "For a director who began his career the year after Arizona and New Mexico were admitted to the Union, the parallel ambiguities of personal and social history project meanings and feelings beyond the immediate association of images. No American director has ranged so far across the landscape of the American past, the worlds of Lincoln, Lee, Twain, O'Neill, the three great wars, the western and trans-Atlantic migrations, the horseless Indians of the Mohawk Valley and the Sioux and Comanche cavalries of the West, the Irish and Spanish incursions, and the delicately balanced politics of the polyglot cities and border states" (p. 15).

Chapter 4. Politics and Self-Knowledge in *The Searchers*

1. Obviously Native Americans had a complex and distinct civilization and cannot in any sense be represented as "natural savages." But Westerns are mythic accounts, much less about history than they are expressions of the American imaginary. In that context, the symbolic role played by Indians, however historically inaccurate, is what is at issue. There are a number of political reasons why it was also important to portray Indians in such a clumsy, stereotypical way, but that would be a separate discussion.

2. A somewhat simplistic example of this frequent trope: Martin Ritt's *Hombre*.

3. He still has his sword, so it seems he was fighting somewhere, and he is wearing uniform pants. As in the Civil War, he was also fighting for the "wrong side." For a filmic treatment of the post–Civil War role of mercenaries in Maximilian's Mexico, see Robert Aldrich's entertaining 1954 *Vera Cruz*.

4. I don't mean to suggest that there is a strict congruence between the conditions relevant to understanding a character in a film (or a novel) and understanding a person "in real life." There are important differences. But there is also some overlap, and that is all I need for the moment.

5. See the helpful discussion by Lehman (2004), pp. 239–63.

6. John Carroll has suggested that it is better to view Ethan's attitudes as more "tribalist" than racist, that his hatred is more the product of the Comanche wars than racism as such. See his discussion in Carroll (2004), pp. 239–46. But Ethan's deep mistrust of Martin from the very beginning (and he clearly doesn't think in military terms, as if Martin might be disloyal or a spy) and his bitter remark in the Army hut that life with Indians is not living seem to go well beyond such tribalism.

7. The issue is raised in a particularly dramatic way later in a tense confrontation between Ethan and the Indian chief Scar. They both speak some of the other's language and both, remarkably, have blue eyes.

8. Peter Bogdanovich raised the issue most clearly with Ford himself in a famous exchange. See his (1967), p. 93

9. Cf. Schmitt (1996), p. 36: "all significant concepts of the modern theory of the state are secularized theological concepts not only because of their historical development . . . but also because of their systematic structure."

10. At least the tension and palpable frustration in their scenes together make it clear to me. One sometimes hears it suggested, though, that they had had an affair and that Debbie is its product.

11. The fact that Debbie begins her sojourn with Scar on a grave has suggested to some that she is taken to the land of the dead, and Ethan's journey is a *katabasis*, a mythic descent into hell. See Clauss (1999), pp. 2–17.

12. As in the movie's theme song, which asks "What makes a man to wander?"

13. Almost all of the domestic scenes and, oddly, some of the attack and violence themes force on the viewer the question of the film's use of humor. One is tempted to treat it as typically Fordian, the domestic pleasures and familial warmth, the dancing and music and intimacy that all the struggle and war are for. But it is also possible to see the humor as Brechtean, to borrow a term from Gil Perez. The fact that, as the Rangers begin their assault on a village full of noncombatants, there is all this comic by-play between the minister and the lieutenant about the latter's sword, and the sudden shift in Ethan from maniacal searching to joking sarcasm, does also seem deliberately off-putting, to suggest a level of insensitivity and blindness that alienates us from their "world."

14. In other Westerns, for example in Ralph Nelson's 1966 *Duel at Diablo,* there appears to be an assumption in the white settler society that any adult woman captured by Indians should be able to, and is duty-bound to, commit suicide rather than "submit." The contrast with white men having sex with Indian women (as long as they don't marry them), and the stupidity of such a double standard, is explicit in the film.

15. This is a scene right after Ethan has almost succeeded in killing Debbie. The two searchers are recuperating from an attack by Scar's men, and Ethan has Martin read out a new will he has written in which he disowns Debbie and, remarkably, leaves everything to Martin, even though Martin is no "blood kin," as Ethan has often reminded him. This could have been a powerful scene, the first crack in Ethan's racist commitments. But the power of the scene is undermined by Hunter, whose performance as Martin is

not up to this moment. Hunter has one emotional register throughout the film: eager, intense, emotional involvement. Hawks said
that he was always worried about Wayne as a leading man, that he
had such screen presence that he could "blow away" other actors,
and that is certainly what happens here.

16. Cf. the discussion in Brian Henderson (2004), pp. 47–73.
Henderson also makes some good points about the effect of his
complicated status on Martin's behavior. He cannot aggressively or
even actively court Laurie; he is passive and almost feminized, and
must be pursued, as if he would be a threat if more active. And he
must act out his loyalty to whites more than anyone else (p. 71).

17. Such a reading is not impossible, but I don't think it is correct. If it were right, we would expect a very different (and more
welcoming and reunifying) homecoming than we get. What we get
is a deeply sad and somewhat broken Ethan walking away from the
"white" world.

18. I borrow this example from Nomy Arpaly's interesting book
(2004). See also R. Pippin (2007) for more discussion of this example.

19. Nugent (1956), scenes 231 and 232. The scenes are both
more brutal and the actions more (simplistically) explicable in Nugent's script. Ethan prepares to shoot Debbie, and says, "I'm sorry,
girl. . . . Shut your eyes." And then, after they stare at each other, he
says, "You sure favor your mother" and helps her up.

20. Nugent (1956), Scene 239. In the shooting script, Ethan really has become kindly Uncle Ethan. He rides in, holding a sleeping
Debbie. This is how Nugent describes the final scene.

> He smiles and puts a finger to his lips—
> cautioning her against waking Debbie—and then he rides
> by. Laurie looks then at Martin. He doesn't know whether
> to smile or not; he just waits. And then she is beside
> him and she steps onto his stirruped foot and vaults up
> beside him, and she kisses him just as she had on the day

he left the graves to take up the search. And still holding her beside him, he rides slowly after Ethan and Debbie toward the house.

21. And we should recall that, while perhaps many have lusted after their brother's wife, and many wives might have felt some pull to respond, the somewhat careless and public display of Ethan and Martha at the beginning of the film has to count as reckless and no doubt guilt-producing. It is certainly "noticed" (by being so deliberately ignored) by the Reverend Clayton.

22. Früchtl (2004) reports that a Western is often referred to in German by a word with no English equivalent in discussions of film: *Heimatfilm* (p. 53).

23. See Früchtl (2004) on "die dunkle Kehrseite des heimeligen Glücks" (p. 61).

Chapter 5. Conclusion

1. The film was made all the more poignant, given that the main character is dying of cancer, by the fact that Wayne himself was dying of cancer.

2. Perez (1988), p. 241.

3. At the other end, one might say, of this American Dream fantasy, a record of the experience of its death and the collapse of such a sense of possibility, are Hollywood films noir of the forties and early fifties. Or so I argue in a forthcoming book, *Agency and Fate in American Film Noir.*

4. Jacques Tourneur's great 1947 noir with this name is also a variation of the aging or ex-gunfighter theme, again played with great finesse by Mitchum.

5. Ray says this in a lecture at Vassar, filmed as part of Wim Wenders's 1980 documentary *Lightning over Water.* For a fuller citation, see Eisenschitz (1993), p. 185.

6. In the most well-known example from Ray's films, *Rebel Without a Cause*, the attempt by the teenagers to create an "alternative world" is all at once compelling, touching, and doomed. It also prefigures the attempt at the counterculture coming in the sixties, where politics especially became gesture, resistance, "the great refusal." I am grateful to Bo Earle for discussions and suggestions on this issue.

7. Peckinpah's *Ride the High Country* begins in a similar way and treats a similar theme. Joel McCrea's character, the ex- and aging lawman Steve Judd, enters town and proceeds down the street lined with people gesticulating at him, and so he acts as if there were a parade going on for him, a genuine town-taming hero. But he is as irrelevant to the town as he suspects he has become (the crowd is gesticulating to get him *out of the way;* the Keystone Kops uniformed police call him "old-timer" and "old man"), and it is a gathering to watch a race between a camel and some horses (fraudulent because at the distance set, the horses cannot win), and we are then introduced to a carnival with many Wild West themes. Judd meets an old friend, Gil Westrum (Randolph Scott, who plays a more comical and relaxed character than in his many Boetticher films), who is in a kind of Buffalo Bill get-up, complete with wig, running a shooting gallery and pretending to be the Oregon Kid. The film then explores whether the old virtues of loyalty and what Judd calls simply "respect" and "self-respect" can survive in the new world, whether the two ex-lawmen are aging relics in more ways than one. Peckinpah's answer is complicated, and as with many of his films, there is an undercurrent of barely managed violence, especially male sexual predation and violence, that is so ugly that it is depressing to sit through. The psychological grip of the need to feel "justified," as Judd says, is put under great stress in the film, but, remarkably, it survives, even appears important to the lowest moral strata, the nearly cartoonishly evil Hammond brothers. (The suicidal

eruption of "outlaw honor" at the end of *The Wild Bunch* makes much the same point.)

8. Whatever the trajectory suggested by this reflective take on the West as theater, it reaches a kind of mad apotheosis in Altman's *Buffalo Bill and the Indians*. Or the elegiac and tragic dimensions of Ray's film return for that famous "second time," this time as farce.

BIBLIOGRAPHY

Agel, H. (1961). "Le Western," *Études Cinématographiques* 2, nos. 12–13: 240–366.

Anderson, L. (1984). "John Ford" in Lyons (1984), pp. 158–62.

Anthony, P. D. (1977). *The Ideology of Work* (London: Tavistock).

Arpaly, N. (2004). *Unprincipled Virtue: An Inquiry into Moral Agency* (Oxford: Oxford University Press).

Bayertz, K. (1981). "Hegel und der wilde Western," *Dialektik, 2: Hegel—Perspektiven seiner Philosophie heute:* 138–41.

Bayertz, K. (2003). "Zur Ästhetik des Westerns," *Zeitschrift für Ästhetik und Allgemeine Kunstwissenschaft* 48, no. 1: 69–82.

Bazin, A. (1971). *What Is Cinema,* vol. 2 (Berkeley: University of California Press).

Bazin, A. (1971a). "The Western, or the American Film *par excellence,*" in Bazin (1971), pp. 140–48.

Bazin, A. (1971b). "The Evolution of the Western," in Bazin (1971), pp. 149–57.

Beane, W., and W. Doty, eds. (1976). *Myths, Rites, and Symbols: A Mircea Eliade Reader,* vol. 2 (New York: Harper Colophon).

Blake, M. (2003). *Code of Honor: The Making of Three Great American Westerns* (Lanham, Md.: Taylor).

Bogdanovich, P. (1962). *The Cinema of Howard Hawks* (New York: John B. Watkins).

Bogdanovich, P. (1967). *John Ford* (Berkeley: University of California Press).

Böhringer, H. (1998). *Auf dem Rücken Amerikas: Eine Mythologie der neuen Welt im Western und Gangsterfilm* (Berlin: Merve Verlag).

Böhnke, M. (2001). "Myth and Law in the Films of John Ford." *Journal of Law and Society* 28, no. 1 (March): 47–63.

Bordwell, D. (1971). "The Man Who Shot Liberty Valance," *Film Comment* 18: 19–20.

Braudy, L., and M. Dickstein, eds. (1978). *Great Film Directors: A Critical Anthology* (New York: Oxford University Press).

Browne, N. (1975). "The Spectator-in-Text: The Rhetoric of Stagecoach," *Film Quarterly* 34, no. 2: 26–38.

Brunkhorst, H. (2006). "The Man Who Shot Liberty Valence— Von der rächenden zur revolutionären Gewalt," *Paragrana: Internationale Zeitschrift für Historische Anthropologie,* Bd. 15, 1: 159–67.

Budd, M. (1984). "A Home in the Wilderness: Visual Imagery in John Ford's Westerns," in Lyons (1984), pp. 163–67.

Buscombe, E. (1988). *The BFI Companion to the Western* (New York: Da Capo).

Buscombe, E. (1992). *Stagecoach* (London: British Film Institute).

Cameron, I., and D. Pye (1996). *The Movie Book of the Western* (London: Studio Vista).

Carroll, J. (2004). *The Wreck of Western Culture: Humanism Revisited* (Melbourne: Scribe).

Cawelti, J. (1971). *The Six Gun Mystique* (Bowling Green: Bowling Green University Popular Press).

Clauss, J. (1999). "Descent into Hell: Mythic Paradigms in *The Searchers*," *Journal of Popular Film and Television* 27, no. 3 (Fall): 2–17.

Coetzee, J. M. (1988). *White Writing: On the Culture of Letters in South Africa* (New Haven: Yale University Press).

Cook, P., and M. Bernink (1999). *The Cinema Book,* 2nd ed. (London: British Film Institute).

Cowie, P. (2004). *John Ford and the American West* (New York: Henry N. Abrams).

Darby, W. (1996). *John Ford's Westerns: A Thematic Analysis, with a Filmography* (Jefferson, N.C.: McFarland).

Day, K. (2008). "'What Makes a Man to Wander?': *The Searchers* as a Western *Odyssey.*" *Arethusa* 41: 11–49.

Dworkin, R. (2000). *Sovereign Virtue* (Cambridge: Harvard University Press).

Eckstein, A. M. (2004). "Introduction: Main Critical Issues in *The Searchers*," in Eckstein and Lehman (2004), pp. 1–45.

Eckstein, A. M., and P. Lehman, eds. (2004). *The Searchers: Essays and Reflections on John Ford's Classic Westerns* (Detroit: Wayne State University Press).

Eisenschitz, B. (1993). *Nicholas Ray: An American Journey* (London: Faber and Faber).

Eyman, S., and P. Duncan, eds. (2004). *John Ford: Le pionnier du 7e Art, 1894–1973* (Cologne: Taschen).

French, P. (1973). *Westerns* (London: Secker and Warburg).

Früchtl, J. (2004). *Das unverschämte Ich: Eine Heldengeschichte der Moderne* (Frankfurt: Suhrkamp).

Gallagher, T. (1986). *John Ford: The Man and His Films* (Berkeley: University of California Press).

George, R. A., ed. (1968). *Studies in Mythology* (Homewood, Ill.: Dorsey).

Gleason, P. (1980). "American Identity and Americanization," in Thernstrom (1980).

Grant, B. K. (2001). "Two Rode Together: John Ford and John Fenimore Cooper," in Studlar and Bernstein (2001), pp. 193–219.

Grant, B. K., ed. (2003). *John Ford's Stagecoach* (Cambridge: Cambridge University Press).

Hämäläinen, P. (2008). *The Comanche Empire* (New Haven: Yale University Press).

Hegel, G. W. F. (1969). *Werke in zwanzig Bänden*, ed. E. Moldenhauer and K. Michel (Frankfurt am Main: Suhrkamp).

Hegel, G. W. F. (1975). *Lectures on Fine Art*, trans. T. M. Knox, vols. 1 and 2 (Oxford: Oxford University Press).

Henderson, B. (2004). *"The Searchers:* An American Dilemma," in Eyman and Duncan (2004), pp. 47–73.

Hillier, J. (1985). *Cahiers du Cinéma. The 1950s: Neo-Realism, Hollywood, New Wave* (Cambridge: Harvard University Press).

Hirschman, A. O. (1977). *The Passions and the Interests: Political Arguments for Capitalism Before Its Triumph* (Princeton: Princeton University Press).

Hutt, W. H. (1939). *The Theory of Idle Resources* (London: Cape).

Jung, C. G., and Kerényi (1949). *Essays on a Science of Mythology: The Myth of the Divine Child and the Mysteries of Eleusis* (Princeton: Princeton University Press).

Kahn, V. (2004). *Wayward Contracts: The Crisis of Political Obligation in England (1640–1674)* (Princeton: Princeton University Press).

Kallen, H.M. (1924). *Culture and Democracy in the United States* (New York: Boi and Liveright).

Kirk, G. S. (1970). *Myth: Its Meaning and Function in Ancient and Other Cultures* (Cambridge: Cambridge University Press).

Kitses, J. (1969). *Horizons West* (Bloomington: Indiana University Press).

Kitses, J., and G. Rickman, eds. (1998). *The Western Reader* (New York: Limelight).

Koch, G. (2006). "The Man Who Shot Liberty Valance: Eine Rechtserzählung," *Paragrana: Internationale Zeitschrift für Historische Anthropologie*, Bd. 15, 1: 159–67.

Lehman, P. (2004). "The Limits of Knowledge in and of *The Searchers*," in Eckstein and Lehman (2004), pp. 239–63.

Leutrat, J.-L. (1995). *L'Homme qui tua Liberty Valance: John Ford, Étude critique* (Paris: Édition Nathan).

Liandrat-Guigues, S. (2000). *Red River* (London: British Film Institute).

Luhr, W., and P. Lehman (1977). *Authorship and Narrative in the Cinema: Issues in Contemporary Aesthetics and Criticism* (New York: Putnam).

Lusted, D. (2003). *The Western* (Essex: Pearson Education).

Lyons, R., ed. (1984). *My Darling Clementine: John Ford, Director* (New Brunswick: Rutgers University Press).

McBride, J. (1996). *Hawks on Hawks* (London: Faber and Faber).

McBride, J. (2001). *Searching for John Ford: A Life* (New York: St. Martin's).

McBride, J., and M. Wilmington (1975). *John Ford* (Cambridge: Da Capo).

Maranda, P., ed. (1972). *Mythology: Selected Readings* (Middlesex: Penguin).

Middleton, J., ed. (1967). *Myth and Cosmos: Readings in Mythology and Symbolism* (Austin: University of Texas Press).

Nachbar, J., ed. (1974). *Focus on the Western* (Englewood Cliffs, N.J.: Prentice Hall).

Nugent, F. S. (1956), *The Searchers,* revised final screenplay. http://www.aellea.com/script/searchers.html

Pearson, S. A. (2007). "It Is Tough to Be the Second Toughest Guy in a Tough Town: Ask the Man Who Shot Liberty Valance." *Perspectives on Political Science* 36, no. 1 (Winter): 23–28.

Peary, G., ed. (2001). *John Ford: Interviews* (Jackson: University of Mississippi Press).

Pechter, W. (1978). "John Ford: A Persistence of Vision," in Braudy and Dickstein (1978), pp. 344–58.

Perez, G. (1998). *The Material Ghost: Films and Their Medium* (Baltimore: Johns Hopkins University Press).

Perkins, V. F. (1965). "Cheyenne Autumn," *Movie,* Spring.

Perkins, V. F. (1993). *Film as Film: Understanding and Judging Movies* (New York: Penguin).

Pippin, R. (2007). "Can There Be 'Unprincipled Virtue'? Comments on Nomy Arpaly," *Philosophical Explorations* 10, no. 3.

Rawls, J. (1971). *A Theory of Justice* (Cambridge: Harvard University Press).

Rieupeyrout, J.-L. (1964). *La grande aventure du Western: Du Far West à Hollywood* (Paris: Les Éditions du Cerf).

Rivette, J. (1953). "On Imagination" in Hillier (1985), pp. 104–6.

Rothman, W. (2003). "Stagecoach and the Quest for Selfhood," in Grant (2003), pp. 159–77.

Rousseau, J.-J. (1986). *The First and Second Discourses, Together with the Replies to Critics and Essay on the Origin of Languages,* ed. and trans. Victor Gourevitch (New York: Perennial Library).

Sarris, A. (1962). "Cactus Rosebud, or *The Man Who Shot Liberty Valance,*" *Film Culture,* Summer.

Sarris, A. (1975). *The John Ford Movie Mystery* (Bloomington: Indiana University Press).

Schmitt, C. (1996). *The Concept of the Political* (Chicago: University of Chicago Press).

Sharrett, C. (2006). "Through a Door Darkly: A Reappraisal of John Ford's *The Searchers.*" *Cineaste* 31, no. 4 (Fall): 4–8.

Simon, S. (2003). *The Invention of the Western Film: A Cultural History of the Genre's First Half-Century* (Cambridge: Cambridge University Press).

Slotkin, R. (1973). *Regeneration Through Violence: The Mythology of the American Frontier, 1600–1800* (Norman: University of Oklahoma Press).

Slotkin, R. (1985). *The Fatal Environment: The Myth of the Frontier in the Age of Industrialization, 1800–1890* (Norman: University of Oklahoma Press).

Slotkin, R. (1998). *Gunfighter Nation: The Myth of the Frontier in Twentieth-Century America* (Norman: University of Oklahoma Press).

Smith, H. N. (2005). *Virgin Land: The American West as Symbol and Myth* (Cambridge: Harvard University Press).

Studlar, G. "'Be a Proud, Glorified Dreg': Class, Gender, and
  Frontier Democracy in John Ford's *Stagecoach*," in Grant
  (2003), pp. 132–57.

Studlar, G., and M. Bernstein, eds. (2001). *John Ford Made
  Westerns: Filming the Legend in the Sound Era* (Bloomington: Indiana University Press).

Thernstrom, S. (1980). *Harvard Encyclopedia of American
  Ethnic Groups* (Cambridge: Harvard University Press).

Tillman, J. (2007). "*High Noon* and the Problems of American
  Political Obligation," *Perspectives on Political Science* 36,
  no. 1 (Winter): 39–45.

Tocqueville, A. de (1969). *Democracy in America*, ed. J. P. Mayer,
  trans. G. Lawrence (Garden City, N.Y.: Anchor).

Tomkins, J. (1992). *West of Everything: The Inner Life of Westerns* (New York: Oxford University Press).

Truffault, F. (1955). "A Wonderful Certainty," in Hillier (1985),
  pp. 107–10.

Turner, F. J. (1996). *The Frontier in American History* (New
  York: Dover).

Walker, J., ed. (2001). *Westerns: Films Through History* (Rout-
  ledge: New York).

Walker, J. (2001a). "Captive Images in the Traumatic Western:
  The Searchers, Pursued, Once Upon a Time in the West, and
  Lone Star," in Walker (2001).

Walzer, M. (1996). *What It Means To Be an American: Essays on
  the American Experience* (New York: Marsilio).

Walzer, M. (2004). *Politics and Passion: Toward a More Egalitarian Liberalism* (New Haven: Yale University Press).

Warshow, R. (1998). "The Westerner," in Kitses and Rickman (1998), pp. 35–48.

Weber, M. (1994). *Political Writings* (Cambridge Texts in the History of Political Thought), ed. Peter Lassman, trans. Ronald Speirs (Cambridge: Cambridge University Press).

Weber, M. (2002). *The Protestant Ethic and the Spirit of Capitalism and Other Writings*, ed. Peter Baehr, trans. Gordon C. Wells (London: Penguin Classics).

Williams, B. (2005). *In the Beginning Was the Deed* (Princeton: Princeton University Press).

Wills, G. (1997). *John Wayne's America: The Politics of Celebrity* (New York: Simon and Schuster).

Wilson, G. (1986). *Narration in Light: Studies in Cinematic Point of View* (Baltimore: Johns Hopkins University Press).

Wollen, P. (1984). "Structural Patterns in John Ford's Films," in Lyons (1984), pp. 168–73.

Wood, R. (1971). "Shall We Gather at the River? The Late Films of John Ford," *Film Comment*, Fall.

Wood, R. (2006). *Howard Hawks* (Detroit: Wayne State University Press).

INDEX

Page numbers in *italics* indicate illustrations.